GLOBAL SOCIETIES

GLOBAL SOCIETIES

To Accompany

Bryjak and Soroka

Sociology: Changing Societies in a Diverse World
Fourth Edition

prepared by
Grant Farr
Portland State University

with

Corie Hammers
Portland State University

Allyn and Bacon
Boston ■ London ■ Toronto ■ Sydney ■ Tokyo ■ Singapore

Printed in the United States of American

10 9 8 7 6 5 4 3 2 1   03 02 01

CONTENTS

PREFACE

Global Societies is a supplemental reader to accompany *Sociology: Changing Societies in a Diverse World,* Fourth Edition, by George J. Bryjak and Michael P. Soroka. Bryjak/Soroka has always offered one of the broadest perspectives of any introductory text, with a special focus on the forces of globalization and modernization that are transforming entire societies and contributing to many of the momentous events occurring in the world today. The "Focus On" boxes in every chapter of the Fourth Edition highlight a particular society or region, and offer a detailed analysis of a significant facet of life or pressing issue facing its citizens. Instructors who wish to provide additional opportunities for their class to examine the diverse and dynamic state of societies in the world today can order Bryjak/Soroka packaged together with a free copy of *Global Societies.*

Global Societies gives a brief overview of contemporary social life in eight different countries: Japan, Mexico, Brazil, China, Poland, Iran, South Africa, and Indonesia. The authors chose countries that represent contrasting forms political, social, and cultural organization, and that are in varying stages of moderization. For each society, the authors provide:

- A statistical "snapshot."
- A discussion of the major social institutions, key social locators and processes, and of the most pressing social issues.
- A relevant news article with accompanying discussion questions.
- A list of resources (books, videos, Websites) for further study.

For information on how to order *Sociology: Changing Societies in a Diverse World,* Fourth Edition, by Bryjak/Soroka, with *Global Societies,* contact your Allyn and Bacon representative.

JAPAN

BASIC DATA

Population	126,182,077
Population Growth Rate	0.2 %
Per Capita GDP	$23,100
Life Expectancy at Birth	80.11 years
Form of Government	Constitutional Monarchy
Major Religions	Shintoism and Buddhism
Major Racial and Ethnic Groups	Japanese 99.4 %, Korean 0.6%
Colonial Experience	Never Colonized
Principal Economic Activities	Services 60%, Industry 38%

INTRODUCTION

Japan is an Island chain in the area of the world called East Asia. It lies between the North Pacific Ocean and the Sea of Japan, east of the Korean Peninsula. The three largest Islands are Hokkaido in the North, Honshu, the largest Island with the majority of the population, and Kyushu in the South. Numerous small Islands are also part of Japan. The total land mass of Japan is slightly smaller than the State of California. Japan's population is estimated to be over 125 million. Since the land is mountainous, with Mt. Fujiyama the highest peak at 3,776 meters (over 12,000 ft.), the population is concentrated on the coastal plains. Japan is a constitutional monarchy and has been independent since 660 BC. The monarch is Emperor Akihito.

Japan is ethnically and linguistically homogeneous. Ninety-nine percent of the population are ethnic Japanese; less than one percent are ethnically Korean. There is a small population of aboriginal people in Japan, called Ainu, who live mostly in the southern part of the Island of Hokkaido. The Ainus' physical features are more "Caucasian" than the typical Japanese and they are thought to be the remnants of an earlier population on the Islands that eventually mixed with the East Asian immigrants to make what are now the Japanese people. Japanese is the dominant language in Japan, and is even spoken among the small Korean population. Eight-four percent of the Japanese observes both the Shinto and Buddhist religions. There is a small Christian community.

JAPANESE SOCIETY

Although Japan is an industrialized nation it still retains elements of traditional Asian society. Among the important characteristics of Asian society are strong collectivist values, as opposed to the individualistic values found in the West. In the collectivist value system, the collective good, be it the family, the village, or the factory work group, is put before the good of the individual. At the family level, this means obligations to support extended family members, especially elderly parents, are important. In Japanese industry, company success is put above individual success. Japanese corporations are sometimes pictured as extended families, in which employment is for life and the worker/employer bond resembles the child/parent bond.

This strong sense of the collective good over the individual good results in strong pressure on individuals to conform to group standards. Japanese are often unwilling to speak against the collective for fear of ostracism. For instance, Japanese students are reluctant to state individual opinions in the classroom, but due to modernization these traditional values are in some ways changing in Japan. Today, due to the weakening economy, Japanese industries are forcing people to retire early. In addition, a significant aspect of Japanese culture is the acceptance of idiosyncratic behavior and dress, particularly among the youth.

Another aspect of the collectivist value system is the emphasis put on codes that prescribe proper social behavior. Ritualistic behaviors, such as bowing or using proper forms of address when speaking to elders, show that one is aware of the group norms. The Japanese language, unlike American English, distinguishes between polite and causal usage, so that when speaking to a superior one would uses quite different language forms than one would use when speaking to an equal.

SOCIAL STRATIFICATION AND INEQUALITY

Japan is a relatively affluent country. There are two characteristics of the social stratification system in Japan that make it different than in other industrialized countries: there is less inequality in wealth between the classes; and status or prestige differences are more important than money or power differences. For instance, manufacturing employees make about $34,263 according to a 1992 study, while the same type of workers in the United States make $27,606 (Perrin, 1993). On the other hand, executives in Japan make an average of

$390,723, while American executives average $717,237. In other words, Japanese manufacturing workers make more than American workers, while Japanese executives make considerably less than American executives. The ratio between workers and executive salaries in the United States is about 12 to 1; in Japan it is 4 to 1. Thus the wealth is more evenly distributed in Japanese society than in the United States.

Another way to look at income inequality is to examine the distribution of income to each fifth of the population. In Japan, the bottom fifth of the population receives about 8 percent of the national income, while the top fifth receives about 36 percent. In America the poorest fifth receive less than 5 percent of the national income, while the top fifth receives over 45 percent. In short, in Japan there is less inequality, at least in the distribution of income, compared to most other industrial countries.

The second characteristic of the Japanese stratification system is the emphasis placed on honor or status. The upper class in Japan may not have the level of wealth that the upper class in the United States have, but these wealthy Japanese families have greater prestige and status than do their U.S. counterparts. In terms of absolute wealth, only 7 Japanese were listed in Forbes Magazine's "richest one hundred people", compared to 42 American citizens, and of the ten richest people in the world, five are from the United States and none are from Japan. Yet these prominent families are venerated in Japanese society and referred to with great reverence and respect. In the United States, we assume that the wealthy are just like us, except that they have more money, which we resent.

POPULATION

Japan is approaching a population crisis. However, unlike the crisis of too many children in previous periods, the new impending population crisis is because of too few children. Although the Japanese population is still growing, albeit at a very low rate, 0.2 percent in 1999, the total fertility rate, that is the number of life births a women will have over her lifetime at current birth rates, is 1.48, one of the lowest in the world. To put it in other terms, the average Japanese family is having less than 1.5 children. This is considerably below replacement level, about 2 children per family, and means that the Japanese population will soon begin to shrink in size.

However, this crisis will not be caused by the decline in the overall population size, but will occur because of the changes in the age structure of the Japanese population. Not only does Japan have a very low birthrate, but Japanese also live long lives. The average Japanese citizen born today can expect to live about 80.11 years, which is the highest average life expectancy in the world. (The average life expectancy in the United States is 76.7 years.) Low birthrates coupled with long life expectancies mean fewer children for the present generation, which in turn leads to fewer workers for the next generation to support the increasing numbers of old people. It is estimated that by 2015, 25 percent of the Japanese population will be over 65 years of age, the highest percentage of older people in the world.

Another way to look at the problem is to examine the dependency ratio. The dependency ratio is the ratio of the population of non-working age to those of working age. In other words, it is how many people in the population are "dependent" on those who work. The dependency ratio in Japan by 2015 is estimated to be 64.5 percent, which will be the highest dependency ratio in the world. In other words, for every one hundred people of working age in Japan, there will be over sixty-four people who are not of working age and who depend on those who are. This large number of elderly people coupled with a small number of workers does not bode well for the Japanese economy and for Japanese society as a whole.

FAMILY

Japanese families have two distinguishing characteristics; the family structure is patriarchal and the preferred form of household is extended. The family structure is also patrilocal and patrilineal. In the traditional Japanese family, the man is the head of the household. He is expected to support the family and in turn, it is expected that the other members of the household, the women and children, will give him respect and deference. In the traditional family, it is common for several generations to live in the same household. The eldest son is expected to continue to live in the parent's household with his family. This form of extended family is called a "vertically" extended household, as different from the "horizontally" extended households found in the Middle East.

In modern Japanese society the traditional household is changing, largely due to urbanization. Since the cities of Japan have high density levels, space is limited and typical Japanese houses or apartments are small. In many Japanese contemporary homes or apartments there is no longer space for an extended family to live in one household, and most Japanese now live in nuclear family settings.

GENDER ROLES

There is much misunderstanding and mythology about gender roles in Japanese society. Japanese women are depicted in the Western media as geishas or courtesans, dressed in traditional kimonos, performing the tea ceremony or serving sake to rich men. The truth is somewhat different than the myth. In traditional Japanese society women are expected to be subservient to men, with the additional expectation to marry and to be obedient wives and mothers. When a woman marries, she becomes part of the husband's family and moves into his household. In addition, women are discouraged from holding careers. Although many young women work, they are expected to stop working when they marry.

Dating has become common in Japan, although many couples still meet at an *omiai,* a formal meeting arranged by an interested third party. In the past, the *omiai* took place in the residence of the third party, but now it often takes place in a private room of a fancy restaurant. The parents are usually at the *omiai,* and if they are not, they are introduced to the new bride or groom early on.

It has often been reported that Japanese husbands and wives live quite separate lives. Men often hangout together after work, golf with their buddies on the weekend, and in general spend little time with their wives. Women also have their separate activities. In a survey of several nations around the world regarding the importance of sex in marriage, only 35.3 percent of Japanese couples reported that sex was important in a marriage. In the same survey, over 75 percent of American couples reported that sex was important in a marriage. On the other hand, the Japanese divorce rate is low. In a 1988 study of divorce rates around the world, the Japanese rate was 1.3 divorces per 1000 people in the population, the second lowest after Italy. The divorce rate in the United States was 4.8, the highest in the world. Of course, divorce rates do not tell the whole story. Low divorce rates are often a result of restrictive laws or social norms that strongly discourage or even forbid couples from splitting up. As a result, a low divorce rate may mean that women are forced to stay in unhappy marriages.

Strong gender biases exist in the Japanese working world as well. While more and more Japanese women are entering the workforce, they have not been able to penetrate the upper levels of the professional or industrial world. Most of the Japanese professions are still largely the domain of men. In many industries, unlike their male counterparts, women are made to wear uniforms and are treated like clerical workers even when they have an advanced education.

URBANIZATION

Although Japan has traditionally been a rural country, Japanese cities have always played a major role in Japanese society and culture. The core of Japanese culture and power was always in the cities, which housed the palaces and forts of the nobility. City dwellers are thought to be more sophisticated than country folk in Japanese culture. In modern Japan, 78 percent of the population now lives in urban areas, slightly higher than the percentage of Americans who reside in urban areas, 77 percent. Since Japan has a large population with limited land on which to build, the cities of Japan have high density levels.

Two large urban areas dominate Japan. The largest of these is Tokyo and its surrounding area, which the Japanese refer to as the Kanto area. This metropolitan area has a population of more than 20 million, which makes it one of the largest urban areas in the world. One out of every five residents of Japan lives in the Kanto area. The second largest urban area in Japan is made up of the cities of Osaka, Kobe, and the ancient city of Kyoto. The Japanese call this urban area Kansai.

In modern Japan, density and the resultant high property values poses a dilemma for many Japanese workers. Since most jobs are in or near the major cities, workers have the choice of living in the city near their work where space is limited and property values high, or commuting long distances to live in cheaper, less crowded areas. Thus it is very common for some workers in Japan to either commute to work, which can take up to two hours one way, or to rent very small cell-like apartments in the cities nearer to work. These cell-like apartments, called *danchi* in Japanese, often hold a family of three or four in 500 or 600 hundred square feet, about the size of a small one-bedroom apartment in the United States.

ECONOMY

Japan is one of the wealthier nations of the world and has become a major industrial power since the Second World War. Today it is the second largest economy after the United States. With a highly skilled workforce, good government—industry cooperation, a strong work ethic, and low spending on national defense, Japan was able to grow strongly in the decades after World War II. Japanese industries in automobile manufacturing, electronics, computers, steel production, and shipbuilding are among the best in the world. In addition, Japanese workers are paid well compared to workers in other countries and Japan enjoys a large and prosperous middle class. Japan has a low inflation rate, which was estimated to be .9 percent in 1998. Only 4.4 percent of the Japanese workforces are unemployed.

However, after several decades of growth, the Japanese economy has been in a major recession. This slowdown began in 1992 when over-inflated stock and real estate values fell. This caused industrial production to fall, and, although it picked up some in 1996, the recession deepened in 1997–1998 due to the severe downturn in the Asian economy where Japan was heavily invested. In 1998 the industrial growth rate fell 6.9% from the previous year. These financial difficulties in Japan centered on a banking crisis, a rigid corporate structure, and an inflexible labor market.

By 2000 the Japanese economy seemed to be picking up, along with the Asia economy in general, but long term problems in the banking industry, fixed labor cost, and the aging of the Japanese population will continue to pose challenges to the long term viability of the Japanese economy.

SOCIAL PROBLEMS

On the surface Japan appears to be a country with few problems. Crimes rates in Japan are lower than most industrial countries, there are few divorces, guns are virtually non-existent, the AIDS infection rate is low, unemployment is low, there are very few births to single teenage mothers, the literacy rate is high, and the Japanese have the longest life expectancy in the world. However, social problems do exist and are a concern to Japanese citizens.

Comparing crime rates is tricky, even within the United States, since definitions of crime and reporting differences can lead to very misleading comparisons. However, some statistics can be insightful. The murder rate in the United States has been falling, but stands at 9.4 murders per 100,000 in the population in 1992. The murder rate in Japan at the same period was 1.2 murders per 100,000. Another revealing statistic is the percentage of the population who has been victimized by a crime. In the United States, 28.8 percent of the population report that they have been victimized by a crime, while in Japan only 9.3 percent report that they have been the victims of a crime

Despite these two figures, social problems are growing in Japan. There has been an increase in youth street gangs, called *bosozoku*. While these Japanese gangs do not engage in the same level of violent behavior as American youth gangs, they nonetheless have become worrisome in Japan for their street parties, motorcycle races on city streets, and general rowdy behavior. These youth also represent a new phenomenon in Japan, namely youth who have not done well on national aptitude tests and are therefore shut out of college admissions, which in turn makes it difficult to find good employment.

Organized crime is also a problem in Japan. At least as notorious as the Mafia in the United States are Japanese organized crime syndicates called the *yakuza*. The *yakuza* are involved in illegal activities such as gambling, drug trafficking, prostitution, and extortion. As opposed to American organized crime, they very seldom use violence in their activities, although the use of guns and other violence is increasing.

RACE AND ETHNICITY

Japan is a racially and ethnically homogeneous society. Ninety-nine percent of the population are ethnic Japanese. As a result, there is not a great deal of discrimination towards minority groups, because there are very few minorities. Of course, this does not mean that Japan is free from racism. Racial discrimination is apparent in Japan on a number of fronts. For one, Japan attempts to keep foreigners out of the country, what has been called the "Island Fortress" mentality. Japan, for instance, has been criticized by world relief agencies for not accepting its share of the world refugees and political asylum seekers. In 1990 Japan accepted 2 asylum seekers, while the United States took in over 100,000.

There are minorities in Japan, the most notable being the ethnic Koreans. There are over one million people of Korean descent in Japan and they have faced considerable prejudice and discrimination. Before WWII, Koreans were forced to take Japanese names and they have generally been barred from important jobs and high positions. In addition, Korean youth have a much higher high school dropout rate, and tend to end up in blue-collar jobs. As a result, as with most minority groups, they suffer from low self-esteem and are considered by the Japanese to be inferior. It should be said, however, that the climate in Japan is improving for the Koreans. For instance, almost 50 percent of the Korean marriages are with Japanese, up from 10 percent during the period immediately following WWII.

MODERNIZATION

In its own way Japan is a modern country fully integrated into the new global world. The Japanese have high rates of phone use, most homes have televisions and modern appliances, the Japanese own computers and other high tech gadgets, many Japanese travel abroad, and Japan receives many international tourists each year. In addition, Japan is often on the cutting edge of new products in consumer electronics or cars, and Japan is a leader in modern transportation with high-speed trains connecting Japanese cities.

Yet despite Japan's acceptance, even leadership, of the modern world, there is also a traditional side to Japan that holds modernization at bay. This traditional part of society is rooted in the importance of family and attitudes towards the collective values that has allowed Japan to modernize, but not lose its traditional heritage and culture. To some of the world's developing countries, Japan is a positive role model, since Japan is a testimony to the fact that a country can simultaneously modernize and industrialize, but still maintain its cultural values and ways of life. To put it another way, Japan has modernized, but not westernized.

SUMMARY

Japan is an Island country in East Asia with more than 125 million people and the world's second largest economy. Japan is a racially and linguistically homogenous country in which over 99 percent of the population are Japanese. Japanese values emphasize the collective good over the individual wants and these values lead to strong family and corporate loyalties. Japanese live longer on average than any other nations and with their very low fertility levels will soon find their population size declining and the dependency ratio increasing. By 2015, Japan will have a higher percentage of people over 65 than any country in the world. Japan has large metropolitan areas, with the Tokyo metropolitan area, called the Kanto area, one of the largest in the world. Because of high density rates and high property values in the cities, workers must either commute great distances or live in tiny apartments in the city. Japan is also an affluent society, with less social inequality than found in the United States. The Japanese, however, hold their wealthy families in great respect. The Japanese economy has been in a decade long recession. Japan faces a number of challenges, but continues to have a low crime rate and a low rate of violence. Japan has been able to become a modern country, yet has held on to some of its traditional values and culture.

READINGS

Introduction

This article, ''Gizmoland, Rage for the Machine'' discusses Japan's current obsession with technology. Everything from robot dogs, to automated vending machines, cell phones, walkmans, automated pornography and handheld video games are now the rage in Japan. But what are the consequences. On the one hand, it decreases the amount of face-to-face interaction between people, but on the other hand, these gadgets allows the Japanese to connect with others without having to actually talk to a person. In the past, the Japanese often used go-betweens to make contact with others, now they can do it with a machine. Is Japan putting too much emphasis on technology?

Reading

Larimer, Tim. "Gizmoland, Rage the Machine." *Time Magazine*. 5/1/2000, pp 1–5.

Study Questions

1. Explain how the Japanese fascination with high tech gadgets relates to what you know about Japanese culture?
2. Even though the Japanese have embraced some aspects of technology, they have been slow to embrace the Internet. Why do you think this is?
3. In the past the Japanese have often accepted some aspects of modern life, while retaining core Japanese values. Is that happening in this case?

RAGE FOR THE MACHINE

By Tim Larimer

The simple wooden house sits in an unremarkable old neighborhood in an Osaka suburb, the kind of place people forget still exists in modern Japan. There are no pachinko parlors or cyber cafes—no shops of any kind, really. It's an unlikely place to download the next version of Japan's technological evolution. But listen to what happens when a gray-haired, asthmatic septuagenarian named Kazuko Komiyama returns after visiting friends: "Welcome home," a voice chirps. "Isn't it a nice day?"

The high-pitched greeting belongs to a robot. It's a simple machine, to be sure. This isn't the Terminator, or whiny gold-plated C-3PO of Star Wars, or even Japan's own Astro Boy with his atomic-powered rockets. But it's a robot nonetheless: a chocolate-brown wombat that eventually will be able to flutter its eyes when Komiyama, 77, enters the room and giggle when she scratches its fuzzy little head. It tells her what the weather is like. It reminds her when it's time to take her medicine. It serenades her.

For Komiyama, a mechanical companion is a guard against the dreadful loneliness many elderly Japanese must endure.

She saw one such tragic story on a TV news show recently. "An old man's death went unnoticed because he lived alone," she says. "Day after day, his diary read, 'I didn't meet anybody today. Again.' I don't want to end up like that." So when welfare workers from the Osaka suburb of Ikeda asked for volunteers to test the prototype of Matsushita Electric Industrial Co.'s pet robot, she jumped at the chance. She keeps the robot propped up on a stack of clothes in her living room. After a month, she's starting to warm to the thing, despite one irritating habit. "It speaks with a childish voice," she complains. "That makes me feel like I'm treated as an old person. I would rather have an equal relationship with a robot."

This is modern Japan, a Gizmo Nation where even grannies make friends with their gadgets. For half a century, the Japanese have made it a cultural mission to turn out—and obsess over—a succession of cool, elegant and increasingly human machines. And what machines they have become: chart-topping virtual pop stars; robotic geishas; memory sticks the size of a thumb to carry around video images; headgear that projects computer screens into thin air in front of wearers' eyes; washing mahines for the human body; toilets that measure a person's weight, body fat and urine sugar levels. The country that gave the world transistor radios, the Walkman and hand-held videogames is now positioned to turn its love of gadgetry into a lucrative national enterprise once again.

When the E0, a humanoid robot developed by Honda, took its first unencumbered step in 1986, it was heralded as a major breakthrough. That first step took 30 agonizing seconds to complete. Japan's technological ascent was much less halting, as it embraced machines that would carry it from the depths of postwar despair to the heights of affluence with the speed of a bullet train. Along the way, Japanese put machines on a pedestal, cherished and befriended them. It sounds quaint now, this idea that redemption is to be found in technology. But that was a critical message for Japan to digest back in the 1950s, and it persists as a national mantra today.

It is one of the nation's enduring ironies that this obsession was ushered in by the worst technological nightmare humans have yet created, the atomic bomb. Dropped on Hiroshima and Nagasaki, the devices brought a horrific end to World War II and left Japan dazed, defeated and devastated. The grim reality of what had been wrought by the world's finest minds could easily have predisposed the nation to abhor science, to flinch from technology. But the A-bombs had the opposite effect. "Japanese realized that the only way to live after experiencing the worst form of catastrophe through technology was to become friends with technology," says Saya Shiraishi, a cultural anthropologist at Kyoto Bunkyo University. "People entrusted their hopes and dreams to the machines of the future world."

That decision was not entirely instinctive. In September 1945 Emperor Hirohito, shamed by defeat, explained in a letter to his 12-year-old son Akihito that Japan's military had over-emphasized martial spirit and neglected science. Instead of acknowledging the folly of war, or the horrors that Japan's ruthless army had perpetrated in Asia, the Emperor and Japan's postwar leaders decided that they would embrace the victor's strength—the edge in technology enjoyed by the U.S. The Americans who helped rebuild Japan gave weight to this idea, supporting a manufacturing revolution because the U.S. needed the country to serve as a bulwark against communism.

By the end of the 1950s, Japan had embarked on a campaign to entrance housewives with what became known as the "three holy durables": washing machines, refrigerators and vacuum cleaners. It worked. Japan's factories had kicked into high gear, and its consumers, made richer by new assembly-line jobs, were demanding what the factories were making. Japan had found a way to increase its production and its consumption at the same time, a guarantee of economic growth. For better or worse, machines were now linked to Japan's future.

No less influential than industrial policy or the musings of an Emperor may have been the comic-book character Astro Boy. Appearing in 1951, the robot drawn by Osamu Tezuka quickly became a cultural icon in Japan—a figure that embraced both scientific know-how (he could fly and had super strength) and human frailty (he suffered when his scientist father banished him for failing to grow up). "Astro Boy represented hope for Japan at a very difficult time," says Junichi Murakami, sub-director of a museum near Osaka that honors Tezuka. "He emphasized science, not nature, because he wanted people to get rich from science." Even the robot's name—in Japan, he's called Tetsuwan Atom—turned destructive technology into another word for salvation. "Astro Boy was like our religion," says Minoru Asada, an Osaka University robotics researcher. "The robot was never something to be feared."

Today, those bonds have never been stronger, as Japanese live in an increasingly automated world. Use a pay phone and an image of a uniformed woman appears, bowing. There is a train line that runs without human operators, ticket-takers or conductors. Vending machines sell an amazing array of goods: beer, 10 kg bags of rice, fried octopus balls (cooked while you wait), videogames, porn magazines. There are robots that run factories by themselves, robots that make parts for other robots, even robots that make sushi. It's not unusual to see scenes like this one at a Tokyo restaurant: a dozen people sit down to dinner, each with a sleek notebook computer plugged into a cell phone. They don't talk much. They e-mail each other, and other friends who can't join them in the restaurant. The diners— all fans of an actress they have never met but with whom they have communicated online—need the laptops to connect, even when sitting across a dinner table from each other.

Recently in a hot springs town near Nagano, 101 owners of Aibos, those pet robot dogs made by Sony, got together to compare notes and see how their "pets" would react in a crowd of robotic canines. They dressed their Aibos in little coats and hats and brought them in fancy wicker cases designed for real dogs. Wataru Hiraishi, 35, prowled the convention with a laptop computer, equipped with a camera and connected to his cell phone. He was broadcasting the event live over the Internet. "Yes, I talk to it all the time," Hiraishi says of his own Aibo. "I say, 'What are you doing?' But it never responds."

Common sense suggests that there's something unhealthy about an obsession with a robot dog, or any other machine for that matter. But in Japan, these gadgets serve an important social purpose, linking people who have been disconnected in an impersonal, urban world. Single people looking for a mate can use a video-cell-phone matchmaking service. Men wanting more illicit companionship use telephone clubs that allow them to select a woman's picture, dial her up from a phone booth and arrange to meet. In video arcades, you can anonymously challenge players at other consoles to games without ever speaking to them. "Among Japanese there's an interesting combination of social reserve and a strong urge to network, to make friends," says Kim Binsted, an artificial-intelligence researcher at Sony. "People use the gadgets to overcome their reserve and make contact."

There is a history to this cultural impulse. In the old days, says Masayuki Iwata, head of planning at cell-phone matchmaking firm Kekkon Joho Center, "an auntie-type would get a fee for introducing people." Auntie that has 1 million subscribers in Japan. The program's main feature is the cartoon character a user can transmit along with his or her e-mail. "People prefer intermediaries over face-to-face communication," says Hachiya.

This all sounds like a strong argument for Japanese to embrace the Internet. Yet oddly, Japan has been slow to log on—14% of Japanese use the Net, less than half the percentage in the U.S. The explanations are familiar: personal computers are not popular because it's difficult to use the Japanese alphabet on a keyboard; telecommunications charges, among the highest in the world, make Internet access prohibitive; the industries that drove the development of information technology in the U.S.— banks, insurance companies, finance firms- have in Japan enjoyed protection from competitors. Therefore, they have had little incentive to become more efficient.

That should change now that trade and investment barriers have been lifted- opening previously protected sectors to foreign competition. Moreover, the gateway to the Internet is moving from the personal computer to a more Japanese device, the cell phone. Already, 41% of se-

nior high-school students in Japan carry mobile phones to school, compared with 12% in the U.S. "People are getting comfortable walking around with their own information systems at hand," says Yuichi Washida, an analyst at the Hakuhodo advertising agency's research institute.

But are any of these tech-crazed kids learning how to create new technology? After a decade-long slump, Japan needs to muster all the tech savviness it can to revive itself yet again. Yet the next generation seems interested more in consuming technology than producing it. Robotics researcher Shuji Hashimoto, a Waseda University physicist, says he grew up in the 1950s viewing scientists as heroes. Today, nearly half of junior-high school students surveyed by the Ministry of Education said they dislike or hate science class.

At the same time, schools are cutting back on science training. Junior-high students underwent 420 hours of science instruction annually in 1970. Today they get 350 hours, and in three years, that number will be reduced to 290. High-school students in Japan receive about half the science instruction their British counterparts get. The Japanese education system was once known for its discipline and high standards; today there is a dumbing-down of the curriculum by lowering standards and drastically reducing the content taught in classrooms. One cram school teaches basic biology to medical students, because so few of them have studied the subject in high school. And the old complaints about the education system have not gone away. "In Japan, students are not expected to think," says Fumio Hara, a mechanical-engineering professor at the Science University of Tokyo. "It's all memorization."

Even the Astro Boy generation is becoming disillusioned. "People thought science and technology were almighty and would solve every problem," says Jinzaburo

Takagi, a nuclear physicist. "Now their negative aspects are being exposed and seem instead to be causing the problems." Indeed, the presumed infallibility of science is eroding because of a series of nuclear power plant accidents, polluted waterways, toxic clouds released from trash incinerators and crumbling bridges and tunnels on train tracks. Maybe, Japanese are starting to ask, their technological prowess is not so mighty after all. Even one of Japan's latest marvels, the I-mode cell phone that links to the Internet, is so beset with problems that its operator, NTT DoCoMo, has said it will scale back new subscribers.

In some quarters, the 1990s are being written off as Japan's lost decade. While information technology was transforming the U.S. and the rest of the world, Japan was making super-flushing toilets and Tamagotchi electronic pets. Many Japanese wonder if the country can transform its affection for machinery into a new economy for the 21st century.

They should take comfort in the history of the previous one. Japan didn't invent the transistor. But Sony co-founder Akio Morita was smart enough to buy rights to the device and figure out what to do with it. Flash forward half a century, as Sony uses robotics technology developed in the U.S. as the basis for the Aibo. Now in Japan there is a buzz in the air about robots, dotcoms and video phones, to be sure, but also about dramatic changes in the way people do business that could eventually usher in a new era of entrepreneurism and dismantle the old-boy network.

Even Astro Boy is back, in film revivals and emblazoned on children's lunchboxes. "There's a boom in nostalgia for Astro Boy," says the museum sub-director, Murakami. "The economy has been sluggish, but he always represented hope for the future. If people believe in him, then maybe their dreams will come true again." Japan's faith in technology just might redeem the nation once more.

RESOURCES FOR FURTHER STUDY

Books and Articles

Kerbo, H. and John McKinstry. 1998. *Modern Japan*. McGraw-Hill: New York.

This book is a short and concise sociological examination of modern Japane society. It contains chapters on the major Japanese social institution, as well as discussions on Japanese cities, social problems, social stratification and modernization.

Kriska, Laura. 1998. *The Accidental Office Lady*. North Clarendon, Virginia: Tuttle Books.

This book tells the true story of a Japanese American woman who is assigned as a trainee with Honda. As a woman in a Japanese Corporation, she is made to wear a uniform, the men don't, serve tea and the take the coats of the male executives. She exposes the rigidity of the Japanese corporate cultures and the sexual bias present in Japanese society.

Lebra, Takie Sugiyama. 1993. *Above the Clouds: Status Culture of the Modern Japanese Mobility*. Berkeley: University of California Press.

This book is written by a Japanese-born anthropologist who studies the Japanese aristocracy. This aristocracy was established during the Meiji period and ranked directly below the emperor and his family. Although this group was officially dissolved in 1947, they continue to be perceived in Japan as social nobility.

Reischauer, Edwin. 1990. *Japan: The Story of a Nation*. New York: McGraw-Hill.

This book tells the story of the development of Japanese society by one of the leading experts in this area. The book particularly focuses on Japanese society after WWII and the forces in modern Japan.

Websites

Japan—A Country Study

http://Icweb2.loc.gov/frd/cs/jptoc/html#jp0120

This website includes information regarding Japanese life, history, and culture. This is a United States Library of Congress Website.

World Desk Reference: Japan

http://travel.dk.com/wdr/JP/mJP_intr.htp

This Website offers general country information regarding Japan, including demographics, statistics and other information.

H-Net Asia-Pacific Network

http:/www.h-net.msu.edu/~Japan

This Website offers current news and information about contemporary Japan.

Japanese Information Link

http://www.jinjapan.org

This Website comes from the Japanese Ministry of Information. It provides information on Japanese cultural and social events and also provides links to many other sites.

Films and Videos

Kokoro, the heart within, by Scott Featherstone. Lorien Productions; BWE Video, Bountiful, UT (1998).

This documentary is a detailed account of the Japanese way of life and its culture. Japanese social customs, the social life, and Japanese civilization are all thoroughly analyzed. Even the spiritual heritage of Japan as well as particular Japanese spiritual traditions are dealt with. Such spiritual elements including nature—the giver of blessings, and the oceans—the lifeblood of Japan give the viewer a powerful understanding of the importance of spiritual life in Japan.

MEXICO

BASIC DATA

Population	100,294,036
Population Growth Rate	1.73%
Per Capita GDP	$8,300
Life Expectancy at Birth	72 years
Form of Government	Federal Republic
Major Religion	Catholic 89%, Protestant 6%
Major Racial and Ethnic Groups	Mestizo 60%, Amerindian 30%, White 9%
Colonial Experience	Colony of Spain until 1810
Principal Economic Activities	Industry 26%, Services 68%, Agriculture 6%

INTRODUCTION

Mexico, officially the United Mexican States, or in Spanish, *Unidos Mexicanos,* is one of three countries making up North America. Mexico is approximately three times the size of Texas and borders on the Pacific and the Gulf of Mexico. On its southern border are the countries of Belize and Guatemala, and on its north is the United States. There are over 100 million people in Mexico. The geography includes both desert in the north and tropical forests in the South. The capital and largest city is Mexico City.

THE SOCIETY

Modern Mexicans trace their heritage to two distinct groups of people; the Spanish conquistadores, and the indigenous Amerindians who lived in this area before the Spanish arrived. Mexicans are proud of this mixed ancestry and the people who identify as descendents of this mixed ancestry make up 60 percent of the Mexican population. The people of this mixed ancestry are called *Mestizos.* In addition, 30 percent of the population are Amerindian, and about 9 percent are listed as White, or European. Most of the population speak Spanish, although many Amerindian languages are spoken in rural areas. The Mexican population is 90 percent Catholic and the Catholic Church plays a major, although at times controversial, role in both the local and national society.

The concept of mestizo mixes conqueror with conquered. Soon after Columbus first sailed to the new world in 1492, the Spaniard Herman Cortez landed in what is now Mexico in 1519 with 508 soldiers and 16 horses. Within a short period of time he and his men managed to conquer and destroy the powerful Aztec nation in the area of central Mexico. Not only did the Spanish conquistadores kill and plunder the native people, but perhaps the greatest plight they brought to Mexico were European diseases, such as Small Pox, which over a very short period of time killed 95 percent of the indigenous population. It is estimated that the population in this area was about 25 million before Cortez arrived, by 1575 it is thought to be about 1.3 million.

Not only did the Spanish conquerors decimate the native population, but they also developed a colonial system in Mexico that enslaved the indigenous people, and stripped and exploited resources from Mexico to enrich Spain. This colonial system was based, in part, on *haciendas,* which were large estates controlled by the Spanish Crown in which local Amerindians worked as indentured peons. By 1821, Mexico was able to free itself from Spanish rule and claim independence.

Mexico has also had a long and, at times, difficult relationship with the United States. The United States annexed Texas in 1845, which was followed by the Mexican-American war. The treaty between the United States and Mexico that followed the war, called the Treaty of Guadalupe Hidalgo, enabled the United States to annex Mexican territory that today includes all of Arizona, California, Colorado, Nevada, and New Mexico, and parts of Utah and Wyoming. For this territory the United States paid 15 million. Two lasting effects of this treaty were that it not only took much of the richest lands away from Mexico, but it also left many people of Mexican heritage within the borders of the United States.

SOCIAL STRATIFICATION

The Mexican stratification system can be roughly divided into three classes, upper middle, and lower classes. The relative positions of these three classes is not uniform, however, in that there is a large gap between the lower class and the middle and upper classes. In addition, there is a significant difference in wealth and income between the rural and urban people, and between regions of Mexico.

Mexico's upper class is comprised of two groups; wealthy urban industrialist and the rich rural landowners. The upper class is characterized by the strong influence of a relative small number of powerful and wealthy families. Not only does the Mexican upper class own much of the productive agricultural land, but whole sectors of the national economy, such as banking, are controlled by a small group of families. The Mexican upper class has strong cultural and economic ties outside of Mexico. Many of the upper class have degrees from prestigious American or European universities, and they invest much of their money outside of Mexico. A high percentage of this upper class claims pure European ancestry.

The Mexican middle class is composed of three groups; white-collar workers in the private and public sectors of the Mexican economy, the new urban professionals, and small businessmen. As in many developing countries, this class has little political or social cohesion, yet provides political and economic stability to the Mexican society. This middle class was especially hurt by the recession in the 1980's and by the dept crisis in the middle 1990's that led to the rapid devaluation of the Peso. The standard of living of the Mexican middle class plummeted and has not recovered.

The Mexican lower class is much larger than the other two classes combined. The lower class is composed primarily of the rural poor and those rural peasants who have moved to the city. They work largely in the informal sector of the economy where government regulations covering work hours, wage rates, or child labor do not apply. Many families among the lower class survive by pooling money and working several jobs simultaneously. Young men among the Mexican lower class often try to find work in the United States, where wages are better. Many of these families in the lower class survive in large part on remittances from the United States.

Rural poverty is a major problem in Mexico. Seventy percent of the poor in Mexico live in rural areas. The poorest regions of Mexico are also the areas with the highest percentage of Amerindians. The poorer states are mostly in Southern Mexico, and the poorest is the state of Chiapas where most of the population are Amerindian. In many areas of this state there are no public services or roads and infant mortality and illiteracy rates are high. As is often the case in developing countries, poverty leads to social and political unrest.

THE MEXICAN FAMILY

One of the great strengths of Mexican society is its strong family structure. Mexican households are traditionally based on patrilineal kinship. Often several nuclear families related on the male side live and work together. Brothers and cousins help each other in a mutually beneficial arrangement. The youngest son is expected to live with his nuclear family in the patrilineal household to take care of the aging parents and the younger remaining siblings. The traditional role for women is to stay home and perform the domestic chores, but in many families, especially among the urban poor, women must work to bring in money for the survival of the family.

With the collapse of the Mexican economy in the 1980's, the Mexican family structure became especially important. Cooperation among family members and the ability of members of extended families to pool resources allowed many families to survive in difficult times. In the informal economy, cottage industries set up by women in their homes produced needed income, while the men either worked in laboring jobs, or tried to find work in the United States.

GENDER ROLES

Gender roles in Mexico are part of a cultural stereotype that is part myth and part reality. In traditional Mexican culture, men are expected to be tough, strong, authoritarian, and sexually virile, a role which is referred to as *machismo*. In this traditional model, women are expected to be patient, to have moral and spiritual strength, and to be virginal and faithful to their husbands. This role is referred to in Spanish as *marianismo*, that is, like the Virgin Mary. In fact, although Mexico is clearly a patriarchal society, there are a variety of gender roles.

Several characteristics mark gender relations in modern Mexico. For one, although women have made dramatic gains in some areas, the ideal role for women is still domestic. There are still clear expectations of appropriate feminine and masculine careers. In addition, the major economic and political positions in Mexican society are dominated by men. Therefore, Mexican women have very few opportunities to gain either political or economic power and independence.

Mexican women, however, play an important role in the workforce. As the economy of Mexico turned down beginning in the 1980's the burden was unequally shouldered by women. Women were forced into the workforce to help families survive. In addition, global restructuring has led to the increased demand for women in certain industries. The *maquiladoras,* factories established on the Mexican side of the U.S.-Mexican border to make products for the United States market with cheap Mexican labor, prefer women workers. Women are often more willing to work for low wages, less apt to unionize, and do not view the work as a fulltime career.

It would not be fair to say that there has been no progress towards more equitable gender roles in Mexico. Women were given the right to vote in 1953, school enrollment for girls is nearly equal to boys, and women are steadily moving into new areas. In the Mexican parliament women hold 17 percent of the seats. In the United States congress, women hold only 12.5 percent of the seats. Declining fertility rates are also freeing women from th   essures of child bearing and child rearing.

POPULATION TRENDS

The Mexican population passed the 100 million mark in 1999. Al   ugh the birthrate has fallen considerably in the last two decades, the popu   on continues to grow and is expected to reach 120 million by 2015. The to   ertility rate, which measures how many children an average woman will   e over her lifetime at current birthrates, was 2.85 in 1999, down from 5.   1975. This indicates that the Mexican population is growing at approxin   ly 1.7 percent annually.

Because of the high fertility rate, the Mexican population has a   eable percentage of young people. Thirty-five percent of the population is u   r the age of 15. On the other hand, Mexico has a low percentage of elderly   ple; only 4 percent of the population is over sixty. The life expectancy is   ears for males and 72 years of age for females, lower than the comparable   ires for the United States, but higher than many other countries at the sam   vel of development. However, infant mortality rates, the number of childre   ho die the first year of life per 1000 births, is still relatively high at approxin   ly 25 per thousand.

URBANIZATION

Like many developing countries, Mexico is experiencing rapid populat   growth in its major cities, particularly Mexico City. Most of this rapid urb   growth is due to the exodus of the rural poor into the cities. In 1975, 62.8 p   cent of the Mexican population lived in urban areas, by 1999 almost 75 p   cent of the population were urban dwellers. In 1980, only seven cities i   Mexico had populations greater than 500,000, but by the year 2000 over 2   cities had populations over 500,000. Mexico City is now estimated to have   population of over 20 million people, making it the largest city in the world.   Border cities on the U.S.-Mexican border have also grown rapidly, in part because of the new maquiladoras. Tijuana, for instance, now has a population of over 1.5 million people.

This rapid urbanization has created enormous problems for Mexico. Mexico City has the worst urban air pollution in the world. According to the World Health Organization, Mexico City had unacceptable ozone levels 320 day out of the year in 1999. Citizens of the city routinely wear gasmasks when outside, and venders sell oxygen on the city streets. Another problems related to rapid urbanization is the critical shortage of housing in many of the Mexican cities, leading to the increase of slums made up of make-shift houses.

ECONOMICS

The Mexican economy is characterized by its close ties to the U.S. economy and on it dependence on petroleum exports. Eight-seven percent of Mexico's exports go to the United States while almost 75 percent of its imports come from the United States. This dependence on American imports and exports leaves the Mexican economy especially vulnerable to swings in the U.S. economy. Dependence on petroleum exports for income also makes Mexico vulnerable to changes in world prices of oil. For instance, when world oil prices rose in the early 1980's Mexico benefited, but when oil prices fell in the 1990's the Mexican economy suffered. Mexico also has a serious external debt problem, estimated to be $154 billion in 1999. Inflation also remains problematic, running at 18.6 percent in 1998.

The Mexican economy has gone through a number of swings. During the 1960's and 1970's the economy grew rapidly and was referred to as the Mexican Miracle. However, by the mid 1980's economic growth had fallen and the standard of living in Mexico began to fall. This downturn continued into the 1990's abetted by the rapid devaluation of the Peso that took place in the mid 1990's. By the late 1990's the Mexican economy was again growing. In 1998 the Mexican economy was growing annually at 4.8 percent, although this growth rate is probably not sustainable.

There are major structural problems in the Mexican economy. Although the per capita GDP was $8,300 in 1998, which is not bad by world standards, there are serious structural imbalances in the distribution of wealth and income. Fifty-five percent of the national income goes to the richest 20 percent of the population. In addition, 25 percent of Mexican families live below the poverty line. The official urban unemployment rate is listed at 2.6 percent, but it is no doubt much higher. In addition, low wages and underemployment continue to exacerbate rural and urban poverty.

RACE AND ETHNICITY

On the surface, Mexico appears to be the model of good race relations. After all, the nation celebrates its mixed-race, mestizo, heritage. A majority of Mexican, over 60 percent, claim mestizo heritage and many government and business leaders are mestizo. In fact, those claiming pure European heritage are sometimes ridiculed for having "forgotten their Amerindian ancestors'. In addition, Amerindian contributions to society and cultures are recognized and honored. But this picture of Mexican race relations belies a more troubled truth.

There are over 57 Amerindian languages still spoken in rural areas of Mexico, and many of these Amerindians continue to live in deep poverty. Amerindians are defined in Mexico for census purposes as those who speak native languages, and not on physical features or lineage. Most Amerindians live in rural areas where they have historically worked as indentured or subsistence farmers. In many of these rural areas of Mexico there are no public services, schools, or, in some remote areas, even roads. Over 80 percent of Amerindians live below the Mexican poverty line. Thus, the cultural and economic gulf between the rural Amerindians and the urbanized mestizo middle class is enormous. As in the U.S., the indigenous population of Mexico makes up the lowest rung of society.

SUMMARY

Mexico is one of three countries that make up North America. It is a developing country with a large population that prides itself on its mixed Spanish-Amerindian culture. As a Spanish colony for many years, it has a strong tie to Spain and Spanish remains the official language of the country. It has a strong traditional culture that continues to defines distinct gender roles, family relations, and cultural values, although these social norms are changing as Mexico modernizes and urbanizes. Although the birthrate has fallen, the country continues to grow rapidly. This growth is particularly seen in the major cities, including the capital, Mexico City. Mexico City is now estimated to be the largest metropolitan area in the world and is suffering from polluted air and urban crowding. Although Mexico prides itself on being a mixed-race country, the living conditions of the Amerindians remains low and discrimination continues.

READING

Introduction

The following article appeared in the **Economist** just prior to the Mexican elections that brought Vicente Fox to office and ended the decades long rule of the Institutional Revolutionary Party. The article describes the current economic and social situation in Mexico, including the economic slowdown, which led the Mexican electorate to vote for change. The article shows that issues of rural poverty, poor education, and inadequate health care continue to plague Mexico and play an increasing role in the national politics.

Reading

"Mexico's Election," *Economist,* June 24th 2000, pp 25–27.

Study Questions

1. The article describes some of the fundamental ills in Mexico. What are these and how do they relate to the election? What do you think the new government in Mexico can do about some of these important issues?
2. The article discusses the growing division in Mexico between the north and the south parts of the country. From what you know about Mexican society, what are the major differences between the north and the south? How can the new Mexican president deal with this division?

MEXICO'S ELECTION: THE BEGINNING OF THE END OF THE LONGEST-RULING PARTY

Christian Villaseñor is a tousle-haired, middle-class 21-year-old who earns 20,000 pesos (around $2,000) a month working as a clerk for a small import company. It is a good wage, he admits; it maintains his habit for cool clothes and a mobile phone. But he saves a lot, and considers himself a world away from the spoilt rich kids who tear around Mexico city's smarter parts in brand-new cars that are washed by their parents' valets every morning. He represents entrepreneurial, would-be modern Mexico, and his vote on July 2nd is probably going to Vicente Fox, the charismatic former businessman who is running for the opposition National Action Party (PAN).

Now consider Rene Magdaleno, a primary-school teacher in his 40s in the southern state of Oaxaca. Mr Magdaleno has a tough job, struggling to teach children whose first language is not Spanish and whose parents try to keep them at home to work in the fields. Yet his wage is only one-third of Mr Villaseñor's. He will vote for Cuauhtemoc Cardenas of the left-wing Party of the Democratic Revolution (PRD), although he knows he has little chance of winning. The narrow favourite for Sunday's election, especially in poor areas like Oaxaca, is Francisco Labastida, the career politician running for the Institutional Revolutionary Party (PRI), which has ruled Mexico for the past seven decades.

Next week's election in Mexico is about divisions: between haves and have-nots, rich north and poor south, between those who want something new and those who cling to the past. It is also about the divide between a newly confident opposition and a ruling party that, while slowly adjusting to a changed world, is still on the defensive and still in thrall to undemocratic ways.

At first glance, Mexico is doing remarkably well, especially considering the dramas of the past decade. In December 1994, when the present president, Ernesto Zedillo, came to power, the country was in grave straits, afflicted by political violence and economic mismanagement: the currency pegged and over-valued, a huge current-account deficit, foreign investment dominated by short-term portfolio capital (most of it taking flight) and $40 billion of debt about to fall due for repayment. Within days of Mr Zedillo's arrival in office, his government was forced into a bungled devaluation that led to the peso's collapse and a deep recession.

Thanks in part to emergency loans from abroad, the economy recovered surprisingly quickly. Mexico's macroeconomic numbers are now the envy of its Latin American neighbours. In the past four years, GDP has grown by an average of 5.1% a year and manufacturing employment by 3%. Inflation, which was running at 52% in 1995, could fall to single figures this year. This admirable record is partly due to good government and partly to the North American Free-Trade Agreement (NAFTA), which came into force in 1994; since then, both trade and foreign direct investment have more than doubled. But, successful as Mr Zedillo's stabilisation policy turned out to be, it caused real wages to fall by nearly a quarter; they have since begun to creep up again, but so far the improvement is hardly visible.

Now, according to government figures released last month, the gulf between the country's rich and poor is wider than ever. Between 1996 and 1998, the share of the national income earned by the richest tenth of households rose from 36.6% to

38.1%. Meanwhile, the poorest 60% of households saw their share fall, from 26.9% to 25.5%. That takes income distribution back to its levels of 1994. According to Miguel Szekely at the Inter-American Development Bank in Washington, during the 1990s inequality in wages increased more in Mexico than in any other Latin American country. Mr Villaseñor, for instance, earns more than five times the national average salary, and some 60m of Mexico's 100m people earn less than a tenth of what he does.

Mexicans may well ask why, if their country is doing well, the general standard of living remains so low. As they go to the polls in a week's time, most will vote on the basis of party loyalty, family tradition, the attitude of their friends, or which candidate looks best on television. A few, though, may reflect on what seven decades of the PRI have brought them, and, above all, on five-and-a-half years of rule by President Zedillo, whose campaign slogan was *Bienestar para tu familia:* "Well-being for your family".

One Party, a Dozen Opinions

"Remember," a new PRI mayor is told, as he is handed a pistol and a copy of the penal code, "you are the representative of the executive, legislative and judicial branches, and you must act as such." This was actually fiction—a scene from "Herod's Law", a recent film set in the 1940s—but, according to older Mexicans, it was pretty close to reality.

For much of its existence the PRI has been less a party than a cronies' network, with no ideology save that of holding on to power. In the past century, few parties can boast leaders as diverse as Lazaro Cardenas (1934–40), who nationalised the oil industry and jump-started one of the world's most ambitious land-redistribution programmes, and Carlos Salinas (1988–94), Mr Zedillo's predecessor, who ended land reform and sold off most of the state's assets. Just last year, a survey of senior party officials found that their ideologies ranged all across the social and economic spectrum.

Like the Soviet Communist Party, the PRI penetrated (and still penetrates) everything. But its genius has been to cultivate loyalty, using repression only as a last resort. It defused political dissent by permitting and even financing it. Instead of rigging elections, it co-opted support so that fraud was often unnecessary. Land redistribution, for instance, became a superb (and not undemocratic) political tool, since it gave parcels of land to millions of grateful farmers.

During the years of statism, this system worked well. But economic mismanagement and a collapse in the price of oil—the government's chief source of revenue back then, and still about a third of it now—prompted an economic opening in the 1980s. Meanwhile, some policies were seen to be bankrupt. Land distribution, for example, split the land into tiny and barren plots farmed by people who were too poor to invest in modern techniques.

At the same time, political dissent grew. Electoral fraud became more blatant and more controversial, culminating in the 1988 presidential election, when Mr Salinas's victory was widely believed to have been fixed. Reforms were required, but the country lacked the institutions to make sure they were properly implemented. Although they talked and sometimes acted like modernisers, Mexico's presidents were still bound by the loyalties of the PRI network.

That generated a schizoid approach to change, of which Mr Salinas's *sexenio* (six-year term) was a perfect example. He was by far the most radical of Mexico's recent rulers—privatising banks, telecoms and other industries, institutionalising open trade with the United States through NAFTA, ending land reform, decentralising power, loosening controls on the media. But many of the reforms were half-measures which, instead of solving problems, only created new ones that became apparent later.

One example was the banks, some of which were sold to Mr Salinas's friends, from whom he and the PRI later called in favours in the form of large donations. Since they were allowed to operate under weak supervision, too many of the banks went on lending sprees that left them with huge bad-loan portfolios after the crisis. Likewise, Mr Salinas sold Telmex, the state telephone monopoly, without first creating a monopolies commission or a telecoms regulator; competitors and the authorities are now struggling to break the giant company's dominance of the market. And he went into NAFTA without fully considering the competition that Mexican farmers would face from their bigger, better-equipped and better-subsidised American counterparts as protective tariffs disappeared. Small maize producers, in particular, are now being wiped out.

By stopping the redistribution of land, Mr Salinas hoped to introduce capitalism to the countryside. He gave farmers who had been granted plots the right to sell them. This generation, showing the deep conservatism that characterises Mexico's peasantry, has proved reluctant to do so. But their children face harsh choices between scratching out a livelihood on a few acres of often poor-quality soil, or migrating en masse to the cities or across the northern border.

Cowboys and Indians

The hardships of small farmers point to another gap that has been growing in Mexico: the one between north and south. The division between Mexico's geographical halves has always been great, but the uneven effects of the changes of recent years have made it worse. The north, close to the United States, has absorbed the lion's share of benefits from NAFTA, such as the *maquiladoras,* factories that import parts or materials to make finished goods for re-export. With these, it has absorbed modern business practices. It is also home to modern farming on big ranches, the kind that is most likely to survive the competition with American producers. The PAN's Vicente Fox, with his plain-talking entrepreneur's manner, is every bit a man of the northern culture.

The south remains poor and rural, as hilly and inaccessible as the north is flat. This is where most of the country's Indians live, many of them subsistence farmers. For decades, the PRI has bolstered its support here with universal subsidies and handouts, though not to much effect. The south still has the worst public services, the lowest levels of education, the greatest number of conflicts over land. Consequently, it also has the most social unrest; any journey through the southern states takes you past roadblocks manned by soldiers who politely (if you are a foreigner) check your bags for explosives.

The social problems of Chiapas, one of the poorest states, lie behind the Zapatist rebellion that began in 1994 and still smoulders on, pitting hundreds of thousands of pro-Zapatist villagers against the army. Smaller guerrilla groups have since popped up sporadically in other southern states.

Less violent left-wing protest, too, has not disappeared. A ten-month strike at the National Autonomous University, and continuing annual teachers' strikes, are signs of an activism which cannot be contained in the only mainstream political force of the left, the PRD. None of these ructions is likely to start a civil war. But they are not being resolved either. PRI governments, so accustomed to command and control, have still not figured out how to deal with protesters except by buying them off, ignoring them or repressing them.

The Zedillo Stalemate

Hopes that the PRI would change in response to all these challenges centred for a time on Mr Zedillo himself. Unlike his predecessors, who manoeuvred their way into the top job, he fell into it when Mr Salinas's hand-picked successor, Luis Donaldo Colosio, was assassinated a few months before the 1994 election.

Mr Zedillo was young, a technocrat, and held a doctorate in economics from Yale. He looked like a new man. Yet he campaigned just like one of the PRI old guard, taking full advantage of heavily biased media and unregulated campaign finance; and, since PRI cronyism means that Mexico has no career civil service, he had to bring his own team of hangers-on into government with him. That is one reason why he was unprepared for the mess that Mr Salinas left behind.

The old web of political connections, though it is being picked apart knot by knot, still exists. And though there is no suspicion that Mr Zedillo is a crook as some of his predecessors were, his reforms have not gone to the heart of the system. One sign of this is his bail-out of various industries and banks. During the recession

of 1995, interest rates of up to 100% made it impossible for many lenders to pay back their debts and turned the already shaky banks into basket cases. Mr Zedillo's government rescued many of them; taxpayers must now pick up the bill, which some estimates put at over $100 billion, or 21% of GDP. They will also have to stump up for smaller bail-outs in industries such as construction and sugar.

Another failure to grapple with the system is the persistence of monopolies or near-monopolies in areas such as telecoms, beer and cement. Although the government is packed with bright young technocrats like Mr Zedillo himself, they clash with members of the old guard who believe in protecting national champions. Furthermore, although big companies may be able to get credit on overseas financial markets, small ones have had to rely on the sickly banks, which have been reluctant to lend ever since 1995. It is no accident that both Mr Labastida and Mr Fox are promising extensive help, such as credit schemes, for small and medium-sized businesses.

Crime, too, has hardly been touched. Mr Zedillo has had to face both a surge in petty crime, which is blamed on the economic crisis, and an increase in organised crime: especially in drug-trafficking, after the relative weakening of the Colombian drug gangs allowed more room for Mexican ones. Crime levels have fallen from their peak in 1997, but clear-up rates remain low, as does public confidence in the police. Some recent changes should improve things, in particular the creation of a national database so that the country's myriad police forces can share information, not only on criminals but on corrupt policemen.

There has not been much progress against the drug gangs either, despite a great deal of help from the United States and a few big arrests. The Mexican government argues, with reason, that the problem will not go away until the United States does something about its own people's fondness for drugs. But part of the cause is also corruption among Mexican officials. There has been a steady trickle of embarrassing, prominent cases.

Lastly, there is the problem of continuing poverty, especially in the south. Mr Zedillo's government is proud of having spent a bigger slice of its budget on social programmes than any other, and of spending it more wisely. It has tried to tackle poverty by ending universal benefits which, like land distribution, were as much aimed at winning the loyalty of the poor as at reducing their poverty. Instead, it is trying to concentrate on those most in need.

Progresa, the main anti-poverty programme, is more forward-looking: for instance, families who get benefits must agree to send their children to school, and the money is handed to the women instead of the men, who tend to drink or gamble it away. The Zedillo government is also starting up projects to help small farmers change their traditional crops for more profitable ones or use their land for something else. It has attracted *maquiladoras* to southern states. The education gap between the richest and poorest states has shrunk. Health has improved. But in the short term, at least, these sorts of adjustments cannot keep pace with the accelerating advantages that rich Mexico has over poor Mexico.

For all that, Mexicans now live in a markedly different country to the one they inhabited six years ago. "Herod's Law" is losing its grip, as institutions shift from being tools of the executive to being checks and balances on it. The Supreme Court can now overturn laws that it deems unconstitutional and rule on disputes between different levels of government. When the PRI lost its majority in the lower house of Congress in 1997, the chamber transformed itself overnight from a rubber stamp into a genuine legislative body—albeit a chaotic one, since the parties have yet to learn the art of political negotiation.

The Leopard's Spots

There is also more openness. The federal budget is published in full these days, and the president's discretionary and quite legal "secret fund", which was said to totalled $900m during Mr Salinas's *sexenio,* has quietly been shrunk to nothing. The press is more querulous, and so more interesting. Unfortunately, Mexicans still hardly read it; the combined circulation of all newspapers, national and local, is around 2m.

Wonder of wonders, even the PRI has become more democratic. Mr Labastida was its first presidential candidate to be chosen not by presidential whim but by a primary election, even though it may not have been perfectly clean. And Mr Zedillo has given autonomy to the Federal Electoral Institute, whose preparations for July 2nd have made election-day fraud virtually impossible.

Yet the prospect of a clean polling day has not ensured a clean run-up. In recent weeks the media, social organisations and foreign observers have denounced numerous cases of vote-buying and coercion. Gifts have been offered in return for the promise of a vote; pressure has been put on union members and state employees to vote for the PRI; PRI literature has been given out with aid to flood victims and struggling farmers. "The federal government's social programmes are PRI programmes," one former PRI cabinet minister has told the media, "and we're going to use them to win the presidency."

There lies the most important political divide. The urban, the young, the well-off and the well-educated are more likely to vote for the PAN; the PRI is still strong in poor and remote areas, where people associate it with the government that has given them handouts for so long. Yet even if it does not happen this year, demography may well prove the undoing of the PRI. By 2006 there will be around 15m new potential voters, many of whom will probably want to shake off the old system. Even if Mr Labastida wins on July 2nd, he may turn out to be the last PRI president of Mexico—at least for a while.

RESOURCES FOR FURTHER STUDY

Books and Articles

Canak, William and Laura Swanson. 1998. *Modern Mexico.* New York: McGraw-Hill.

This book offers a concise discussion of Mexican society from the perspective of sociology. It includes chapters on the Mexican family, economy, social stratification, politics and gender relations, as well as other topics.

Gutmann, Matthew. 1996. *The Meaning of Macho: Being a Man in Mexico City.* Berkeley: University of California Press.

This book reviews the changing gender roles in Mexico. Gutmann argues that it is no longer enough to be a "pistol-packing charro *(cowboy) of yore, looking for a tranquil rancho where he can hang his sombrero." Because of the changing economics, women are playing a more dominant role in Mexican society, and the men must accept this.*

Oppenheimer, Andres. 1996. "Guerrillas in the Mist." *New Republic.* 214(25), pp. 22–23.

This article describes the attempt of the Zapatistas Movement to gain international attention to the plight of the Amerindians in Southern Mexico.

Stannard, David E. 992. *American Holocaust: The Conquest of the New World.* New York: Oxford University Press.

This book chronicles the conquest of the New World, including Mexico, by the Europeans, particularly the Spanish. Before the European conquest the Amerindian population in central Mexico number approximately 25 million, 75 years the Spanish conquest the population was approximately 1.3 million, a decline of over 95 percent. Most of the Amerindians were killed by European diseases, particularly smallpox, typhoid, mumps, measles, and diphtheria.

Websites

Mexico Web

http://mexico.web.com.mx/

Lists general category Websites links that include art, culture, science and technology, computers and the Internet, education, companies, entertainments, events, government, news, personal pages, states, tourism and health.

Stanford University Mexico Web page
http://www-leland.stanford.edu/~flyhigh/
mexico/mexico.html

This site links to Mexican Webpages focusing on history, culture, general facts, and other topics.

EZLN Website
http://www.ezln.org/

This is the website of the Ejercito Zapitista Liberacion Nacional *the official name of the Zapitista movement. This is a movement active among the rural poor Mexican Amerindians, particularly in the Southern region of Mexico. The Website explains their activities and goals.*

Films and Videos

A Day in the life of a Mexican family, by Gregorio Garcia. Troy, MI: Teacher's Discovery (1988).

This film is a videorecording of the Torres Arroyo family in Mexico City. This documentary provides a real life account of a modern day family living in Mexico, thus showing the viewer the Mexican way of life and it's customs, traditions, and typical lifestyles.

BRAZIL

BASIC DATA

Population	171,853,126
Population Growth Rate	1.16%
Per Capita GDP	$6,100
Life Expectancy at Birth	64.06 years
Form of Government	Federal Republic
Major Religions	Roman Catholic 70%
Major Racial and Ethnic Groups	White 55%, Mixed White and Black 38%, Black 6%
Colonial Experience	Colony of Portugal until 1822
Principal Economic Activities	Agriculture 14%, Industry 36%, Services 50%

INTRODUCTION

Brazil, officially the Federative Republic of Brazil, or in Portuguese *Republica Federativa do Brasil,* is located in South America. It borders the Atlantic Ocean, which gives the country an extensive coastline of 4,578 miles. Brazil is the largest country in Latin America with 3,286,470 square miles of land, occupying nearly half of the continent of South America. Its landmass is slightly smaller than the United States, making it the fifth largest country in the world. Besides the Atlantic Ocean, Brazil's border touches ten different countries. These include the French Guiana, Suriname, Guyana, Venezuela, and Colombia, which all are located to the North of Brazil, Uruguay and Argentina to the South, and Paraguay, Bolivia, and Peru to the West. Brazil has a population of approximately 170 million. Currently, the president of Brazil is Fernando Henrique Cardoso. As president he functions as both the chief of state and head of government. Administratively, Brazil is broken up into 26 states and one federal district. Brazil's capital is Brasilia, located in the southern portion of Brazil's central region.

Brazil has a varied climate, including areas classified as equatorial, tropical, semi arid, highland tropical, and subtropical. The areas that receive large amounts of rain, such as the Amazon Basin have verdant and lush evergreen trees, while in semi-arid places such as the northeast, a dry bush predominates. The Pantanal Mato-Grossense, which is also one of the world's largest biological reserves, is a plain located in the western portion of the center of the country made up of tall grasses, weeds, and widely dispersed trees.

In addition to its long coast on the Atlantic Ocean, Brazil contains two river systems that shape its distinctive geography, the Amazon and San Francisco Rivers. Although not as famous as the Amazon, the San Francisco River is the largest river completely within Brazil, flowing over 1,000 miles from the Brazilian Highlands to its confluence with the Atlantic Ocean. It is the Amazon River system, however, that dominates Brazil. The Amazon Basin is considered the largest single reserve of biological organisms in the world. Scientists estimate that there are anywhere from 800,000 to 5 million species living in the Amazon Basin, 15 to 30 percent of all the species in the world. The Amazon Basin also contains many other assets, including valuable minerals and indigenous Amerindian populations.

RELIGION

Approximately 70 percent of Brazilians identify themselves as Roman Catholic. Brazil's strong Roman Catholic heritage can be traced to the Iberian (Portuguese) missionary goal of spreading Christianity to the New World. In the 15th Century the Castilian Pope granted Portugal the rights to this area of South America, with the provision that they convert the local population to Christianity. This conversion, which was more often than not done using force and violence, included the native people of Brazil, that is the Amerindians, and later African slaves.

As is often the case, Brazilians have mixed orthodox Catholicism with local and African traditional beliefs, creating several syncretic religions unique to Brazil. The most well-known and socially acceptable combinations are called *Umbanda* and *Candomble*. This religious mixing has also created a religious practice commonly referred to as black magic, or *macumba,* which can be used for good or evil purposes. Other religions that account for around 3 to 5 percent of the Brazilian population include the Church of the Later Day Saints, Jehovah's Witness, Judaism, and Buddhism.

In the last two decades Brazil has seen the rapid increase in evangelical Protestantism, which has made dramatic advances among Brazils poor. The proportion of the population considered evangelical grew from 3.7 percent in 1960 to 6.6 percent in 1980, while in the 1991 census this proportion had already risen to 19.2 percent, or 28.2 million followers. This raise in evangelical Protestantism is in part do to the perceived failure of the Catholic Church to respond to the needs of Brazil's growing underclass, and, in part, to the well-financed efforts of the evangelical Protestant Organizations in the United States and Europe.

ETHNIC AND RACIAL GROUPS

Brazil, largely as a consequence of its colonial past, has an ethnically diverse society. People of European descent account for 55.3% of the population and thus make up the majority of the population. They are descendants of the European colonialists and conquerors of Brazilian territory. This European population is composed mainly of Portuguese, but also include people of German, Italian, Spanish, and Polish descent. Those of mixed race, mostly European and African, make up almost 40% of the population. People of "pure" African descent make up about 6 percent of the population. Brazil, as opposed to other countries in South America, has a very small Amerindian population which is at less than 1 percent. There are also small populations of Arabs, Chinese, and Japanese in Brazil.

Brazil has a unique pattern of race relations that can be traced to its historical past. The Portuguese, who were the first European immigrants to arrive in Brazil in the 16th Century, made slaves of the local Amerindians to work in the sugar plantations, mines, and later on coffee plantations. The Amerindian labor, however, soon proved to be inadequate, in part because they rebelled against forced labor resulting in several violent insurrections, and also because the Amerindians died in large numbers of diseases brought from Europe, particularly Smallpox. As a result, the Portuguese began bringing slaves from Africa. Slaves provided cheap labor and were less apt to retreat into the local forests.

Brazilian slavery had several characteristics that made it different from slavery in the United States. When slaves were first brought to Brazil, slaves were relatively cheap and the living conditions in Brazil were harsh. As a result, slaves were treated poorly and many died from the harsh conditions. Also, when African slaves first started arriving in Brazil, Brazil still had a relatively small European population. As a result the slaves were able to keep much of their African culture, including language, music, and religious beliefs. This can be seen today in modern Brazil which contains strong and visible components of African culture. Another characteristic of Brazilian slavery was the high degree of miscegenation. The result of this mixing of Europeans and Africans are apparent in the physical features of modern Brazilians.

The Amerindians, on the other hand, were native inhabitants of Brazil. They are estimated to have numbered between 2 and 5 million at the time of first contact with Europeans in the early 16th Century, and were organized into hundreds of tribes and languages. By the early 20th Century this population had dwindled to 150,000, largely due to disease and violence. Today, in large part due to the 1910 Indian Protection Service and later the 1988 Brazilian Constitution, which allows the Amerindians to keep territories they traditionally occupied, the Amerindian population is making a recovery (albeit a slow one) with numbers now hovering around 330,000. Today, this population consists of 230 tribes that speak more than ninety languages and 300 dialects.

The British stopped the African slave trade in the early part of the 19th Century, and soon European immigrants, largely Italians, began arriving to replace slave labor, mainly on coffee plantations. This Italian immigration to Brazil stimulated the flow of other European settlers later in the 19th Century, primarily from Germany and Poland. Most of these European immigrants came to Brazil to establish farming colonies.

The arrival of Japanese and Middle Eastern immigrants in the early twentieth century added to Brazil's racial diversity. The Japanese worked mainly in agriculture, while the Lebanese, Turks, and Syrians became involved in commerce. Today, this Japanese population constitutes the largest community of Japanese outside of Japan and Hawaii.

BRAZILIAN SOCIETY

Modern Brazilian society is a mixture of European, Amerindian, and African cultures. This mixing can be seen in the physical features of the Brazilians, their music, their language, religions, and their societal values. Brazil has sometimes been referred to as a model for other countries trying to cultivate unity through cultural diversity. Brazilians are known for their relaxed attitude concerning official laws and norms, which they regard as imposed from the outside. Brazilians are also reported to have strong beliefs in the "common good" of society, which probably derived from Brazil's harsh colonial past. Since many Brazilians are descendents of slaves, they have strong antiestablishment values that view official laws as the creation of the powerful and therefore do not apply to the common person. At the interpersonal level, Brazilians are conciliatory, tolerant, and cordial.

Brazil calls itself a racial democracy. Race is viewed as a continuum with no distinct categories as in the United States or South Africa. Yet despite this lack of race categories, one cannot help but notice that most of the poor are black and most of the upper class are white.

POPULATION

The population of Brazil was estimated to be at just under172 million people in 1999 and growing at an annual rate of 1.16 percent. The population is expected to reach 200 million by the year 2015. The population growth, as in most countries of the world, has fallen in the last two decades. The total fertility rate, the number of children a woman will have over her lifetime at current birthrates, was 2.28 in 1999, down from 4.5 children in 1975.

Due to Brazil's current birthrate, Brazil has a relatively young population. Those 14 years and younger make up 30 percent of the population. On the other hand, average life expectancy in Brazil is around 64 years. As a result, those in the 65 years of age or older category comprise only 4.9 percent of the population. There is a large discrepancy between women's and men's life expectancy where women in Brazil live a full ten years longer than men on the average, with 69 years for women and 59 years on average for men. There is no clear explanation for this, although it may have to do with differentials in life styles between men and women.

The infant mortality rate, which measures the number of children who die in their first year of life, is 35.37 for every 1,000 live births, high by international standards. High infant mortality rates reflects a high proportion of the rural population living in places with poor health facilities and poor sanitation, especially clean water.

The literacy rate, that is the percentage of people who can read and write, is the same for men and women at 83 percent. While this level of literacy is relatively high, there are, nonetheless, high levels of illiteracy in some areas of Brazil and among some groups. Literacy is low in rural areas where the poorest people live and among the Amerindians and Black populations. For example, a 1991 census revealed that 29.9 percent of all blacks were illiterate, those of mixed race had the second highest rate at 27.4 percent, and whites had the lowest number of people who were illiterate at 11.6 percent.

SOCIAL STRATIFICATION, INEQUALITY, AND THE LABOR FORCE

Despite several decades of economic gains, Brazil exhibits a stratification system with a large gap between the rich and the poor. For instance, Brazil's national income distribution shows that the richest 5 percent of the Brazilian population received almost 37 percent of the national income, while the poorest 40 percent received only 7.2 percent using data from the 1990 census. Brazil also has a large percentage of its population in poverty. Using Brazil's definition of poverty, 17 percent of the population lives below the poverty line. However, using the United Nations definition of poverty as the situation where people live on less than one dollar per day, the percentage of those in Brazil in poverty increases to almost 30 percent. This means over 50 million Brazilians live on less than one dollar per day. Poverty is especially acute in rural areas where almost 43 percent of the residents are listed as poor, compared to 9.6 percent in metropolitan areas, and 18 percent in urban areas.

Brazil suffers from unemployment, although its unemployment rates are lower than most South American countries. In 1998, the unemployment rate was estimated to be 8.5 percent, approximately 5 million people. Even those with jobs, however, may still be in poverty. Approximately 6.5 million people in the employed work force earn less than one-half of the minimum wage, a monthly average of $299.

Many of the poor are in the informal economy. It is estimated that as many as half of the workers in Brazil are in the informal economy, which means they work without contracts or legal recognitions. These jobs are "off the books" and the workers receive no benefits, including health benefits or retirements, and they are generally not paid legal wages. Many of these workers in the informal economy are small business owners, laborers, or seasonal workers in agriculture.

As in most countries, the social economic stratification has implications beyond wealth and income. Wealthier people attend better schools, are more apt to go on to higher education, have longer life expectancies due to better nutrition and cleaner environments, and live in safer neighborhoods.

FAMILY LIFE

As with the economy, there is both a formal and an informal pattern to family life in Brazil. Reflecting both the Portuguese background and the importance of the Catholic Church, Brazilians regard the nuclear family as the basic unit of society. In the formal society, the nuclear family, that is the husband, wife, and children, is also a symbol of civilized life. The Church sanctifies the union between a husband and wife, and most Brazilian children are christened in the Church. Women should obey their husbands and the husbands should support and protect the family. Fidelity and honor are important values in the formal society.

Yet the realities of life in Brazil have led to a different picture of family life. Though they hold family and kinship in high esteem, Brazilians nonetheless often resort to consensual unions and marital dissolutions. Thus, marital separation and divorce, technically forbidden by the Catholic Church, are now common in Brazil. Much of the reality of family life stems from poverty. For instance, many of the poor women are often heads of household, and families often include children from different unions and marriages.

WOMEN IN BRAZIL

Historically Brazil has been a patriarchal society, in which men dominated within the family and in the larger society as well. As in many countries, men were the heads of households, their wives legally subordinate to them. Divorce was illegal, and women were unable to vote. Essentially, women were men's property as were any children they had between them. The legal situation of women began to change and women were given the right to vote in 1933. By 1977 divorce became legal, and by 1988 under the constitution women became equal to men for all legal purposes.

Female participation in the labor force has been growing dramatically. Women made up only 18 percent of the labor force in 1970; by 1990 female economic participation was at 30 percent. The participation of women in the labor force is a mixed blessing. Women are overrepresented in the services sector, where most jobs are low paying and low status. Approximately 70 percent of the women in the labor force are employed in the services sector as compared to 42 percent of men. Women are also underrepresented in the formal sector of the economy where the high paying jobs are located.

There is still a considerable wage gap between men and women. Depending on where one lives, women earn anywhere from 63.5 percent to 77.8 percent of men's wages. Only between 11 percent and 19 percent of this wage differential can be attributed to differences in education and experience. In essence, women in Brazil receive lower wages because they are women.

While inequality still exists, women are gaining on many fronts, including education. There are as many women, if not more, as men in schools, even at the highest levels. One study conducted in 1990 found that over 25 percent of all females employed had finished high school, compared to only 16 percent of males. In addition, professions that were traditionally male domains such as law, medicine, and engineering, are becoming more balanced in terms of gender.

Nevertheless, women still are dramatically underrepresented in government, although the situation is improving. In 1994 women made up only 7 percent of the national Congress. To create a more balanced government, in 1996 the Brazilian Congress enacted a quota system mandating that women make up 20 percent of city councils. This increased the number of women elected and was extended by the Brazilian Congress in 1997 to cover the 1998 general elections.

The women's movement has been active in Brazil. The National Council on Women's Rights was created in the 1980's to promote women's issues. This council, along with the women's movement in general, is responsible for galvanizing societal support against such abuses as domestic violence, sexual abuse, rape, and harassment. Brazil has responded to these concerns by creating special police stations for women. Thus, while women are still underrepresented in many parts of society that are still dominated by men, Brazilian women have been making progress in the last two decades.

BRAZIL'S ECONOMY

Brazil has the largest economy in South America and has well-developed agricultural, mining, manufacturing and service sectors. Nonetheless, after a decade of rapid expansion, Brazil was hurt by the world financial crisis of 1997–1998 and by the end of the 1990's had entered into a deep recession. Brazil has been particularly hurt by the increasing globalization of the world economy in which investors move money and resources quickly from country to country according to perceptions of each countries economic potential. Brazil has been forced to float its currency on the world market and to enact austere financial policies to ensure IMF support.

The service sector accounts for most of Brazil's GDP (Gross Domestic Product) at 50 percent, while industry accounts for approximately 36 percent, and agriculture 14 percent. Brazil has attempted to liberalize its industries under what is called the Real Plan, *Plano Real,* and to reduce governmental regulations. This reduction of governmental protection in the industrial sector was done to stimulate its competitive edge in the world market. In an attempt to increase efficiency both at the local and global levels, Brazil began to privatize state-owned enterprises in the 1980's. In addition, this conversion from state-owned to privately-owned would garner larger profits for government since private enterprises increase tax revenues. At first, privatization was confined only to those firms in financial difficulty. Today, due in part to the Cardoso administration, privatization policy is now a major part of Brazil's economic infrastructure with private enterprises in energy, transportation, and the telecommunications sectors.

By the late 1990's the Brazilian economy remained flat, with growth in the GDP at 0.5 percent. Per Capita GDP, which measures the total national economic output divided by the number of people in the population, was estimated to be $6,100 in 1998. The austere monetary policies have kept inflation at a low rate, and in 1998 was approximately 2 percent.

SUMMARY

Brazil is the largest country in South America, taking up almost half of the territory of South America and most of the Atlantic coast. It also has the largest population in South America, with over 170 million people. Brazil has the Amazon River basin, one of the largest preserves of life in the world. The Portuguese colonized Brazil in the 16th Century and brought to Brazil the Portuguese language and Roman Catholicism. The Europeans also brought African slaves to Brazil to work in the plantations and mines. After several centuries of racial and cultural mixing, modern Brazil exhibits a blend of Europe and Africa. The original Brazilians, the Amerindians, died in large numbers in the face of European conquest and now make up a small percentage of the Brazilian population and live only in marginal areas, largely the Amazon Basin. Brazil's population continues to grow, but its birthrate is falling. The Catholic Church remains important in Brazilian society, although Brazil has mixed Catholicism with local traditions to create new religious sects. Although traditionally a patriarchal society, Brazilians have a relaxed attitude regarding social and intimate relationships. Women have come to play an increasingly important role in Brazilian society and are an increasing percentage of the workforce, educational system, and political bodies.

Although a country with considerable wealth, Brazil also has enormous poverty. Almost 30 percent of Brazilians live on less than one dollar per day. The economy, while still the largest in South America, has entered a steep recession at the end of the 20th Century, in part due to the globalization of the world's financial institutions.

READING

Introduction

The following article, *Analysis: Brazil's 'racial democracy'*, looks at how racism, despite claims to the contrary, continues to be a problem in Brazil. Although Brazil has always presented itself as a "model" for other countries to emulate when it comes to racial unity, Jan Rocha shows how the color of one's skin in Brazil has negative and lasting consequences. For instance, although blacks constitute half the Brazilian population they are largely absent from positions of power, and face higher rates of unemployment, infant mortality rates, and poverty.

Reading

Analysis: Brazil's 'racial democracy,' by Jan Rocha, BBC News.

Study Questions

1. How has Brazil's colonial past impacted and influenced the persistence of Brazil's "racial democracy"?
2. In what ways could the government and Brazilian society redress this racial discrimination?

ANALYSIS: BRAZIL'S 'RACIAL DEMOCRACY'

By Jan Rocha

Brazil is celebrating its 500th anniversary: 500 years since "discovery" or "invasion", depending on whether you were a Portuguese explorer or one of the millions of indigenous peoples who already lived there.

The date has made Brazilians think about their origins, the racial mix of Indians, Africans and Europeans which has produced today's population, and the claim that Brazil is a racial democracy.

No other country outside Africa has such a large black population, about half the total of 160 million, yet blacks are almost totally absent from positions of power—from all levels of government, from congress, senate, the judiciary, the higher ranks of the civil service and the armed forces.

Even in Salvador, the capital and major slave port for nearly 300 years, where blacks make up more than 80% of the population, very few are to be found in government.

And incredibly, up until the 1970s even Salvador's carnival parade was for whites—blacks could only push the floats, not dance around them. That situation only came to an end when a group of blacks set up their own black-only Carnival group, Ile Ayie, meaning big house in Yoruba.

They also started a school to teach black children their own history—about the many slave rebellions, uprisings and quilombos (free territories) set up by runaways—usually excluded from official schoolbooks.

Slave Trade

Up to eight million Africans from all over the continent were brought to Brazil between 1540 and 1850, when the traffic was stopped, although slavery was only finally abolished in 1888.

Most freed slaves were then turned out to become vagrants, homeless, jobless, penniless, while the authorities, alarmed that the majority of the population was now black or mixed race, did everything to encourage European immigration to "whiten" Brazil.

This policy lasted well into the 20th century, until the writings of influential sociologist Gilberto Freyre in the 1930s showed that the country's racial mixture could be seen in a positive light and the idea that Brazil was an example to the world in racial harmony was born.

But in 1946 a Unesco study revealed that while most Brazilians approved of racial tolerance, in practice racial discrimination was widespread.

Fifty years later in 1999, a report by the Minority Rights Group International showed that discrimination had continued: black and mixed race Brazilians still have higher infant mortality rates, fewer years of schooling, higher rates of unemployment, and earn less for the same work.

Black men are more likely to be shot or arrested as crime suspects, and when found guilty, get longer sentences.

Yet there is no national black movement in Brazil, no open racial conflict, no apparent racial tension. Black Americans who live in Salvador say they feel much more at ease there than in the racially divided USA.

One of the reasons for this huge difference between the USA and Brazil is that while in America, race is defined by your ancestors—one drop of black blood makes you black—in Brazil what counts is appearance.

If you look white, or white-ish, then you are white. For black Brazilians it is this very blurring of racial lines that makes it so difficult to fight racism. And paradoxically, offers the chance for Brazil to become a real racial democracy, once it faces up to and takes steps to combat racism.

© BBC News Online

RESOURCES FOR FURTHER STUDY

Books and Articles

Neuhouser, Kevin. 1999. *Modern Brazil.* New York: McGraw-Hill.

  This short book is part of a series written on various societies for sociology students. The book covers the major social institutions in Brazil, including the family, religion, the economy, and politics. In addition, it includes chapters on race and ethnic groups, social stratification, gender roles, and modernization.

Lesser, Jeffery. 1999. *Negotiating National Identity: Immigrants, Minorities, and the Struggle for Ethnicity in Brazil.* Durham: Duke University Press.

This book focuses on Brazil's challenge of creating a nation out of European immigrants, descendants of African slaves, and indigenous Amerindians. The book discusses current racial policies and tensions.

Levine, Robert, ed. 1999. *The Brazil Reader: History, Culture, Politics.* Durham: Duke University Press.

This is an edited book containing chapters on various topics regarding Brazil. The Chapters include Brazil's history, Brazilian culture and politics, and a look at the problems in present day Brazil.

Websites

Brazil Connection
http://www.brasilconncetion.com

This site is a portal into the Brazilian Internet and contains a search engine for links to useful Brazilian sites.

Republica Federativa do Brasil
http://www.brazil.gov.br

This is the official site of the Brazilian government. It has interesting and useful information on Brazil and links to other sites.

Brazil Online
http://www.brazilonline.com

This website focuses on information and links to Brazilian culture, arts, and music. It also has current news from Brazil.

Films and Videos

Indians of Brazil in the twentieth century, by Janice H. Hopper. Washington, Institute for Cross-Cultural Research (1967).

This film depicts the various indigenous cultures and langua in Brazil and shows their unique customs and traditions.

CHINA

Population	1,246,871,951
Population Growth Rate	0.77%
Per Capita GDP	$3,600
Life Expectancy at Birth	69.92
Form of Government	Communist State
Major Religions	Daoism, Buddhism (Officially Atheist)
Major Racial and Ethnic Groups	Han Chinese 91.9%
Colonial Experience	None
Principal Economic Activities	Agriculture 19%, Industry 49%, Services 32%

INTRODUCTION

China, officially the People's Republic of China, or in Chinese, *Zhonghau Renmin Gongheguo,* is one of the oldest and most important countries in the world. China is located in East Asia with a population that consists of over 1.2 billion people, the largest population in the world. Its border touches 14 countries and it has a coastline of over 14 thousand kilometers. China's landmass is slightly smaller than the United States, making it the fourth largest country in the world by area. Within its borders are major deserts, sub-artic zones, tropical regions, and three major river systems. Although China has been a unified country for thousands of years, it also includes over 50 minority groups, largely along its border areas.

CHINESE SOCIETY

During much of China's 3500-year history it led the world in agriculture, crafts, science, and industry. Many of the world's important scientific and cultural developments and inventions came from China. However, the industrial revolution in the 19th Century gave the West clear superiority in military and economic development and the West temporally surpassed China. In the first half of the 20th Century China went through a period of instability marked by military defeat, civil unrest, severe famines, and foreign occupations.

After WWII the Communists led by Mau Zedong took control of China after many years of revolution. The government of Mao Zedong took bold steps to reform China's feudal society by imposing strict rules over virtually all aspects of Chinese life, from the family to the economy. The Communist government transformed Chinese society, but in the process tens of millions of people lost their lives and the economy stagnated. In 1978 Mao Zedong died and Deng Xiaoping became the leader of China. Deng gradually relaxed many of Mao's edicts and began to modernize the Chinese economy. As a result, China's economy has quadrupled since 1978, and the number of people living in poverty has declined markedly.

Modernizing China has been an enormous challenge. Traditional Chinese society was based on an oriental form of feudalism, in which peasants were indentured to land owned by large landowners. The traditional society was patriarchal and the country had been ruled by a series of oligarchic emperors for thousands of years. Despite its ethnic diversity, China has had a strong sense of its history and culture, which continues to shape its present culture and society. Chinese culture and society have two roots; the values of propriety and status that derive from Confucianism, and the values and norms that support the collective good over the individual, especially the family.

POPULATION

China has the largest population in the world at over 1,250 million people (1999 estimate). One in five people in the world are Chinese. However, the birthrate has fallen markedly in the last two decades, largely as a result of austere birth control measures that limit each family to one child. The 1999 population growth rate was estimated to be .77 percent and the total fertility rate, the number of children an average women will have over her lifetime at present birthrates, was 1.8. This means that Chinese families are having children at a rate below replacement level and the population is expected to begin to decline by mid-century.

The live expectancy of a person born today in China is approximately 70 years. As a result of the low birthrate China has a relatively low dependency ratio, that is the ratio of people who are not of working age to those who are.

The dependency ratio in 1997 was 47.8 percent, which bodes well for the Chinese labor force.

China's aggressive family planning measures have dramatically lowered birthrates, but have done so at some cost. Clearly, China needed to deal with its burgeoning population. Even at the present low birthrates, there are 58,000 babies born per day or 40.3 babies per minute. Each year the population continues to grow by about 9 million people. To halt this rapid growth, China instituted a family planning program, based, among other things, on limiting each family to only one child. Local officials or neighborhood committees have strictly enforced this 'one child' rule in many areas of China. This policy has been surprisingly effective in lowering China's fertility rate, but the policy of one child per family has clashed with the traditional desire of Chinese families to have many children and to have at least one male offspring to carry on the family name and tradition. The one child rule means that families whose first child is a girl are not able to have a male child, and thus are unable to ensure that their family name will be passed on. As a result, many couples have tried various means to ensure that their one child will be a boy. These means have included attempting to determine the sex of the fetus and aborting if it is a girl, contacting astrologers, and in some cases female infanticide. As a result there are about 15 percent more males born each year than females, and the Chinese population as a whole has about 7 percent more males than females.

FAMILY LIFE

In traditional China, the family structure was patriarchal and patrilineal. Men dominated family life and the family traced its ancestry along the male line. Extended family groups often lived in the same household and cooperated in economic ventures. Clans and other kin-based organizations have played important roles in Chinese economic and political history as well. Chinese family names are important and children are taught to always bring honor to the family. Marriages were arranged between extended families, and were viewed as exchanges between family groups or clans.

In modern China, the Communist government has tried to alter some aspects of the family life, while leaving other aspects in tact. The early Marxist government saw extended family systems as a vestige of the feudal system. Nuclear families were preferred and couples were encouraged to form unions on their own, without family arrangements. The Communists leaders also attacked familial respect for age. During the Cultural Revolution young people were encouraged to challenge their elders and to report their parents to authorities if they harbored subversive thoughts. This period has past and the modern Chinese family has returned to a more normal pattern. Modernization, urbanization, and modern education have done more to change the nature of the Chinese family than has Communist ideology.

GENDER ISSUES

The change in the role and status of women in Chinese society has been dramatic. In traditional Chinese society, women played a domestic role, were subservient to the male members of the family, and were required to take the name of their husband. Women did not attend school, hold political position, or participate in the economic sector, except in domestic production and small-scale agriculture. In modern China, women play a much more important role, both in the family and in the larger society. Women now enjoy the same rights of possession and inheritance of family property as their male counterparts, and Chinese women, in theory, are now able to control their own contraception and make their own marriage decisions.

Chinese women now participate more actively in the economic sphere. Today it is estimated that women make up 45 percent of the Chinese workforce. Among women aged between 16 and 54 years, 85 percent have jobs, a dramatic change from the past. However, even though women are active in the Chinese work force, women are still restricted to certain professions. Women are encouraged to seek careers in those areas where "famine qualities of tenderness, patience, carefulness and persistence" are important (China, 2000). Thus 95.2 percent of the pre-school teachers are women, 75.8 percent of the handicraft workers, and 74.4 percent of the tailors are female.

China has also made strides in including women in the government. For instance, there are 21,000 women judges, 4,512 women lawyers, 1,200 women diplomats, and 80,000 women police in modern China. Women have gained in education as well. Today, 72 percent of Chinese women are literate, compared to 90 percent of men, and most females of school age now attend school.

RACE AND ETHNIC ISSUES

China is made up of 56 different ethnic groups, many of them with their own language. The majority of the people of China are called the Han Chinese and make up about 92 percent of the population. The Han now live in all parts of China, but they are originally from the middle and lower reaches of the Yellow, Yangtze, and Pearl rivers, and the northeast plain. They speak standard Chinese, often called Mandarin Chinese, which is also the official language of China and one of the working languages of the UN. Most of the other ethnic groups live in the border areas of China, and most, except for the Hui and the Manchu who also speak Mandarin, have their own languages.

As in all countries, prejudice and discrimination towards minorities exists in China. The Han Chinese hold a disproportionate number of important government position, the best jobs, and in general dominate all aspects of Chinese society and culture. Since many of the smaller ethnic groups live in border areas far from the center of China, they are somewhat marginal to Chinese life. Recent secessionist activities among some of these groups who resent the domination of the Han Chinese, have caused Beijing to become more aggressive in controlling political activity in some areas.

The major areas of ethnic unrest are in the Chinese provinces of Xinjiang, the eastern most province, and Xizang, the area that is largely Tibet. The Xinjiang province borders on Moslem Central Asia and is largely populated by the Yugar people. The Yugar are Moslem and speak a Turkic language, similar to the other languages of Central Asia. Their culture is more akin to Central Asia and the Middle East than to China, and far from the Han culture of Beijing. As a result, many Yugar resent the dominance of the Han Chinese and there has been unrest by groups seeking to create their own homeland. The situation in Tibet has a different history, but much of the same tensions. The Tibetan people of Xizang, who are culturally quite different from the Han Chinese, resent the recent influx of Han Chinese into the Tibetan home land and seek to break from China.

ECONOMY

The Chinese economy has been growing sense 1978 and has become one of the largest economies in the world. Chinese leaders have been trying to find a balance between a state-controlled economy and a free market economy. They call their new economic policy "a socialist market economy". On the free market side, China has largely replaced its rural collectives with household responsibility in the agricultural sector, and in the industrial sector has given plant managers and local officials increased authority. It has also allowed the growth of small entrepreneurial businesses and relaxed some regulation regarding foreign trade and investment. This has led to a quadrupling of the Gross Domestic Product, GDP, a measure of the total economic output of a country, since 1978.

Part of China's strategy to introduce a combined state controlled-free market economy has been to designate certain areas of China as free-market zones, while other areas are kept under state control. In 1984 China opened 14 coastal cities to overseas investment. This list was expanded in 1985 and again in 1990. China now has 13 free trade zones, 32 state-level economic and technological development zones, and 52 new and high-tech industrial development zones that operate on the principles of a market economy.

On the state control side, China has continued to keep much of its economy under government control and therefore buffered from free market forces. This side of the economy includes state industries as well as financial and banking institutions.

Despite the economic gains, China's economy suffers from inefficiency, corruption, and low productivity. Nonetheless, the Chinese economy has been steadily growing, and in 1998 reported an official annual growth rate of 7.8. Its inflation rate is low and was in fact negative in 1998. The per capita GDP, a measure of the countries total domestic production divided by the population size, was $3,600 in 1998.

SOCIAL STRATIFICATION

A fundamental tenet of socialism, especially Communism, is that every person should be equal in the economy. As a result, whatever one might say about communist or socialist countries, they have usually developed an economic system that is much more egalitarian with regards to the distribution of income and wealth than are capitalist countries. This is true in modern China, as well, although class differences are now growing as China enters the modern world.

In traditional China, there was an enormous gap between the rich and the poor. During the rule of the Communist Government, however, this gap has markedly decreased. This decrease in inequality was accomplished by the simultaneous implementation of state control of the economy and the disregard of market forces, which inevitably lead to differential incomes where only a privileged few became wealthy. However, the economic reforms begun in 1978, but especially accelerated in the 1990's, moved China towards an economy based on market principles. As a result, inequality in wealth and income is again emerging. Figures show that the richest 10 percent of the households in China receive 30.9 percent of the national income, while the poorest 10 percent of the households receive about 2.2 percent. This is less inequality than in the United States, for instance, but more inequality than one would expect in a country based on Communist principles.

In addition, China has considerable inequality in wealth and income by region and between urban and rural areas. Most of China's industrial and technological development has taken place along the coastal regions. As a result, the coastal regions are considerably wealthier than the central or western regions. In addition, although the life conditions of the rural peasants have improved considerably over the last three decades, there remains a large gap between rural and urban incomes. And this gap is increasing. The average income in rural China is only 40 percent of the average urban income. This large difference has caused a number of major problems for China, including a large migration of rural farmers to the urban areas looking for better wages.

MODERNIZATION

China has been cautious about allowing modern or western influences into its society. This isolationism impulse has several causes. For one, China has always seen itself as a self-contained culture and society, uninterested in the rest of the world. In addition, China for many years after WWII was labeled a rogue state by the West and was therefore ostracized from many world arenas. As a result China turned inward, rejecting the West, which was simultaneously rejecting it.

In addition, China sought for many decades to shield itself from the decadence of modern culture because of its beliefs that the Western ideas were contrary to the ideals of the Socialist revolution. Revolutionary leaders, especially Mao Zedong, vilified the western world, and fought to build a society free of the injustices or inequalities found in the West.

Nonetheless, China is now in the process of opening to the rest of the world, although deep distrust still remains. This opening to the west is, in part, driven by the need to modernize its economy, but it is also driven by new affluence among the Chinese middle class. Such consumer products as televisions, video cameras, and computers are increasingly common in China. The purchasing of cars and motor cycles are growing in a country where at one time everyone rode bicycles.

Today, China sends many students abroad for higher education. Tens of thousands of Chinese students come to the United States or Europe for graduate and technical education. As these students return, they inevitably bring western ways and western knowledge with them.

SUMMARY

China has the largest population in the world and is the fourth largest country by landmass. A traditional country with thousands of years of history, China was nonetheless transformed after WWII by the Mao revolution, which brought Marxist ideology and a Communist based government. The first decades of Communist rule were difficult and millions of Chinese died, but since 1978 China has made dramatic economic and social progress. Traditional Chinese society was family oriented and patriarchal. Marriages were largely arranged, women's lives controlled and confined to the home, and extended kin relations played an important role. In modern China many of these traditional customs have disappeared. China has brought its rapid population growth under control by imposing a one-child rule on couples, although this has lead to a society with a high male to female ratio. China was able to reduce income and wealth inequality through state controls of the economic sector, but inequality is again increasing as state controls have become more relaxed and market capitalist forces are allowed to emerge. There is still considerable inequality between regions, and between rural and urban families. China has traditionally been cautious regarding the outside world, and has been a closed country. However, recent moves to open its economy and the growing demands of the new Chinese affluent middle class has led to the increasing exposure of the Chinese people to the outside world.

READINGS

Introduction

This article discusses China's approach to the Internet. On the one hand, China has invested heavily in the Internet, over $50 billion so far, including laying a fiber-optic grid throughout China. China, however, has not been prepared for the social and cultural consequences of the Internet. The Chinese government had hoped to be able to control the information and content available on the Internet, but this has been virtually impossible. It is now much easier for Chinese citizens to receive international news via the Internet, a situation that the Chinese government does not want. In addition, there has been an explosion of Websites from anti-government and counterculture groups.

Reading

"Wired China: The Flies Swarm In." *Economist.* July 22, 2000. pp 24–28.

Study Questions

1. From what you know about China, why do you think the Internet is causing such uproar? Is the Internet bringing the same kind of changes to other countries?
2. The Internet in China is finding popularity among Chinese women and minority groups. Why is this?
3. How do you think that the Internet will eventually change China? Will the Chinese government be able to control the Internet, or will the Internet control it.

WIRED CHINA: THE FLIES SWARM IN

Travel through China's vast, poor hinterland, and even there you will find it: ordinary Chinese being urged, insistently, to take part in the telecoms and computer revolutions. In some of the most backward cities, consumers are assailed by billboards that weave dreams around mobile phones or the latest Chinese dot.com company. In the countryside, Communist-style slogans painted on village walls promise a better life if households would only get a telephone. And in the down-at-heel town of Wanxian, on the steep banks of the Yangzi river 1,900 km from the coast, a red banner across the main street announces "Breast enlargement by computer".

Everything is possible, it seems, in the information age. It is a notion that is encouraged at the highest levels of the state. Since the early 1990s, China's Communist rulers have continually emphasised the need to create modern telecoms and information industries, where possible with home-bred technologies. By this means, China will vault into the ranks of the prosperous, technology-rich countries.

Ultimately, the leaders hope, success will also be a vote of confidence in the party's own policies, and in particular in its insistence on what it calls a "socialist market economy", in which a strong measure of state guidance prevails. The rise of the Internet in China over the past couple of years, and the possibilities of e-commerce, have only reaffirmed these aspirations, even though the speed of the Internet's development in China has clearly caught the state off-guard.

China's leaders intend to avoid the anarchy that has marked the development of the Internet in the West. Rather, they want the Internet to become a vital engine of national progress, harnessed wherever necessary to the controlling forces of the state. Deng Xiaoping, China's late paramount leader, once said of economic reform that when you open the window, the flies come in. Deng's successors, led by President Jiang Zemin, aim to let in as few flies as possible in the Internet age. The degree to which they succeed will shape not only China's economic development, but also its political future.

To date, the state's plans for information technology have chiefly taken the form of massive investment, nearly $50 billion so far, in telecoms and data-processing hardware. A giant bundle of "Golden Projects" are being built for the purpose, among others, of tying local government more closely to the centre, as well as processing enormous amounts of data about revenues. This, it is hoped, will recentralise power that has been lost to the localities during two decades of economic loosening.

But the Golden Projects also have other potential uses. It is no surprise that the security forces, both military and police, were among the earliest users first of computers and then of the Internet in China, or that the security apparatus was responsible for developing most of China's anti-virus software. With these new investments, any future Chinese government, if it were so minded, could monitor and control China's citizens much more forcefully. The government could, for example, introduce "smart" national identity cards on which personal information would be stored, a high-tech version of the manila-bound dossier that is kept by the Communist authorities on every city-dweller in China.

In addition, since 1993, a fibre-optic grid has been laid across the country. Eight high-capacity lines run north-south, and eight east-west, connecting China's principal cities. That backbone has allowed the state telecoms monopoly, China Telecom, under the all-powerful Ministry of Information Industry (MII), to install new telephone lines at a stunning rate. According to Ross O'Brien of Pyramid Research, a telecoms consultancy that is part of the Economist Group, in 1990 there were fewer than 10m telephone lines in China. Today there are 125m lines, with more than 2m being laid every month. Mobile phones are multiplying even faster, from 5m mobile-phone users in 1995 to over 57m today. More mobile handsets will be sold in China this year than in either the United States or Japan. "Teledensity" in China, at just 11 fixed lines for every 100 people, is still low compared with developed countries. But there will probably be several more years of fast growth, making China the most attractive telecoms market in the world.

The speed with which cities are becoming connected through high-capacity lines has allowed the Internet to surge through Chinese society, even if its use is still clunky and slow by western standards. Growth in that use has outpaced even the spread of fixed and mobile phones, albeit from a lower base. In 1995, there were fewer than 50,000 Internet-users in China. If statistics from the state China Internet Network Information Centre are to be believed, there were 2.1m users at the beginning of 1999 and 8.9m at its end. By the end of this year, the number is expected to be 20m. There are now 48,000 registered domain names in China, three-quarters of them commercial.

This kind of growth makes foreigners slaver. A few companies such as Hughes, Ericsson and Motorola have already prospered in China, despite its coolness to doing business with foreigners, by supplying the telecoms hardware that the country craves. Now foreigners want to profit from the Internet boom by providing software and other services. Already, some $150m of foreign investment has gone into Chinese dot.com companies, mainly Internet content-providers and e-commerce start-ups. Foreign investors like to claim that they are doing their bit to open up closed minds and a closed political system. In April, Bill Clinton went further: he claimed that the Internet, with foreign involvement, would eventually bring democracy to the Middle Kingdom.

Hope and Reality

The first problem with such claims is that all foreign investment in telecoms, content firms and Internet service-providers (ISPs) is still technically illegal, at least until China joins the World Trade Organisation (WTO). So the investment made so far stands on shaky ground. That has not stopped Chinese Internet companies from adopting byzantine corporate structures to allow stockmarket listings overseas, in Hong Kong or on America's Nasdaq, designed to attract foreign capital. But the listings come with health warnings, such as this filing with America's Securities and Exchange Commission by Sohu.com, one of China's prominent Internet companies: "It is possible that the relevant People's Republic of China (PRC) authorities could, at any time, assert that any portion or all of our existing or future ownership structure and businesses, or this offering, violate existing or future PRC laws and regulations." In other words, the statement seems to be implying, you are an idiot if you buy the shares.

When China joins the WTO, possibly later this year, foreign influence in its Internet market will become legal, though with tight constraints. Investment in Chinese content- and service-providers will be limited to 49%, a level judged sufficient by

the government to spur local competitors but not swamp them. And even after WTO membership, the possibilities for commercial involvement in China's Internet will be dogged by the country's backwardness. There is much hype about the potential for e-commerce in China. Yet there is no national payments system for buying goods online, there are few reliable distribution channels for delivering them, and online buyers are not confident about security.

Moreover, the state and the many government agencies competing over Internet development have consistently failed to agree about commercial regulation. So the Internet will continue to operate in a legal twilight. It is no wonder that e-commerce deals are at present running at a mere $20m-40m a year.

Sheer primitiveness aside, the Chinese state has other ways of keeping out the foreign "flies"—from liberalism to democracy to pornography—that will come in with the Internet. Here are the four most important:

State control. Although China encourages a degree of competition among ISPs and content-providers inside China, the number of organisations that can interconnect with the global Internet is limited to just four state-controlled entities, led by the MII. This makes it much easier for the state to control what comes into the country. From time to time The Economist's website is blocked. The sites of the BBC, the Washington Post and CNN are blocked almost continuously, as are overseas sites of human-rights organisations and of the Falun Gong, a spiritual movement that has been condemned, and suppressed, as an evil cult.

Encryption. Late last year, regulations were issued by the new State Encryption

Management Commission that banned Chinese companies or individuals from using foreign encryption software. Foreign businesses were required to register the encryption products they themselves used in China. In theory, that gave the state the means to decode traffic passing through the Internet or between branches of the same business. In practice, the regulations were ill-considered and are ultimately unworkable. The state has since backed down from some of its more absurd demands; but ordinary Chinese are still forbidden to use any foreign-made stand-alone encryption products. They may use only state-approved, Chinese-designed encryption ware, which they must register with the commission. This gives the state a powerful tool for monitoring computer traffic.

Internet policing. Earlier this year, the government became alarmed at the amount of "unauthorised" news appearing on Chinese websites. For instance, the websites of some state-owned publications ran stories taken from the uncensored Hong Kong press about a corruption scandal in Fujian province. As a result, the State Secrecy Bureau (another hitherto unheard-of agency) promulgated "regulations for computer systems on the Internet". These extended the ban on the publication of vaguely-defined "state secrets" to the Internet, including e-mail, bulletin boards, chat rooms and news groups.

Even before the new regulations, the state had been an eager policer of the Internet. The first victim, in 1998, was a computer programmer in Shanghai called Lin Hai. He made the mistake of supplying (possibly quite innocently) a dissident Internet magazine in America, VIP Reference News, with 30,000 Chinese e-mail addresses. He was sentenced to two years'

imprisonment, although he did not serve his full term. Other people arrested for Internet activity include Qi Yanchen, a journalist in Hebei province who had posted excerpts from his book, "The Collapse of China", and four journalists who published e-samizdat last year.

Most recently, on June 3rd, Huang Qi was arrested in Chengdu, the capital of Sichuan province. Mr Huang's website, whose address (www.6–4tianwang.com) makes reference to the date of the still-taboo Tiananmen massacre on June 4th 1989, started as a bulletin board for missing people in China. Over the months, it became a forum for discussion of human-rights abuses that the authorities eventually found too provocative. Mr Huang is likely to be charged soon under the new state-secrecy laws.

News monitoring. In addition, the propaganda department of the Communist Party has drafted new laws touching the publication of news on the Internet. Commercial websites are now barred from hiring their own reporters or from publishing "original" content. Only news that has already been published by a state outlet (such as the People's Daily, the official Communist mouthpiece, or Xinhua, the state news agency) is now allowed.

At the same time, the state media will receive extra government money for web development, reinforcing their dominance of what the Chinese are allowed to read. The regulations have killed the hopes of those web portals that wished to shine by providing original news. Sina.com, for instance, built a name for itself with its coverage of popular reactions to the bombing of the Chinese embassy in Belgrade, in May 1999, opening chat rooms in which people could vent their feelings outside government channels.

Politics by E-mail

These state constraints are powerful, but not comprehensive. The government felt angry but foolish when, in April last year, 10,000 or more followers of the Falun Gong suddenly surrounded the compound in Beijing where the top leaders live. The gathering had been organised in large part by e-mail that the government could not detect. The authorities later closed down China-based sites of the Falun Gong.

In a forthcoming essay in China Perspectives, published in Hong Kong, Eric Sautedé traces hacker attacks on American sites of the Falun Gong back to Beijing's Public Security Bureau. But the state lacks the power to prevent similar gatherings-by-e-mail in future. In fact, the security forces are having trouble hiring bright young net-wizards these days, since they would rather apply their knowledge commercially.

In the case of Huang Qi in Chengdu, online viewers were able to follow his arrest live. He wrote: "The Public Security Bureau has summoned me for interrogation. The road is still long. Thanks to everybody devoted to democracy in China. The policemen are here now. So long." A yellow ribbon has been put up on the site, and many people have posted messages of sympathy, along with attacks on the government. Curiously, the state has not—or not yet—got round to closing down the site.

Other provocative sites remain unblocked, too. The government rails against a London-based organisation that advocates Tibetan independence. Yet its website is still freely accessible from China: evidence of how Chinese organs of state control are often fragmented, inefficient and ill coordinated. And the existence of proxy servers overseas always allows the most determined Chinese surfers to skirt round state control.

There are signs that the Internet is already creating a degree of "living space" that challenges state constraints on young and literate Chinese. Earlier this summer, a young student at Beijing University was raped and then killed on her way back to her dormitory late at night. The university authorities tried to sweep the incident under the carpet, and a domestic news ban was placed on the story. But friends in America of students at Beijing University read about the incident in the overseas media and e-mailed the news back to China. Immediately, the students organised two days of demonstrations. The unrest died down quickly; but many people in Beijing, not least in the Communist Party, worried that it might evolve into political protest, as happened in 1989.

Admittedly, the authorities understand now how university bulletin boards work, and what a danger they are. They tried to contain the incident of the dead girl by cutting the links to other universities' bulletin boards. But students have gone on airing their grievances. Recently, the internal board at another university in Beijing has been seething with anger over an announcement, by the English faculty, that final exams would be postponed and that students would have to take a three-week course to act as escorts for visiting foreign officials. A few weeks later, the training was cancelled and the exams put back on schedule. With better ways of communicating among themselves, students feel they are able to resist that sort of high-handed behaviour.

Exotic Blooms

The Internet is opening the door to other groups, too. Several gay websites are now challenging the Chinese taboo on homo-sexuality, allowing people to communicate and meet in a way that might cost them their jobs, or their freedom, in the real world. One website publishes a map for Beijing visitors showing gay bars and even a public lavatory opposite the foreign ministry. Another, based in Guangdong, encourages communication through chat forums and organised events where "net-friends" can meet face to face. Roger Meng, the site's founder, polices the site to keep off pornographic and other messages that might annoy the government.

Women also have their champions, led by a web company called Gaogenxie, or "high-heeled shoes", a symbol of freedom in China against the traditional bound feet. Again, the site steers well clear of politics. All the same, says Yin Hui, Gaogenxie's editor, it deals with issues that mainland publications avoid: for example, Chinese men's reluctance to use condoms, or people's attitudes to sex. In a society where women are expected to marry young, Gaogenxie also devotes space to the challenges facing single women, including single mothers.

All this, though, does not add up to confirmation of a civil society. The web's new entrepreneurial stars, though they are young, hip and cosmopolitan, cannot be counted on to lead demands for democracy and a more accountable government. After all, the best-known entrepreneurs, such as Edward Zeng of Sparkice, a chain of Internet cafés and now a budding dot.com, and Jack

Ma of Alibaba.com, a business-to-business exchange that matches international demand for Chinese products with their suppliers, still have close links to the state, even if they rarely wear ties and would look at home in Silicon Valley. Who would risk their business prospects by allowing provocative content on their sites? A powerful streak of self-censorship pervades Chinese websites. All of them employ what Patrick Horgan of Apco, a consultancy, describes as a "chat-room mama" to strike out sensitive topics, such as Taiwanese independence or democracy, whenever they pop up.

Besides, as part of a new consumer culture in China, the Internet can act as opium for the masses, dulling political desires. The government understands well the effects of the consumerism drug. In the years after Tiananmen, shop windows full of desirable goods did much to divert attention from political dissent.

The present generation of 17–30-year-olds appears much less politicised than the previous one. Is it any coincidence that it is also the generation that is most wired? The state claims that the typical Internet surfer spends 17 hours a week at the terminal. An unscientific wander through the Internet cafés and campuses of Beijing suggests that much of that time is spent logging on, playing games and writing frivolous e-mails to friends sitting across the hallway. The government is probably right in assuming that this is not—at least not yet—a revolutionary generation with a sharp new weapon.

RESOURCES FOR FURTHER STUDY

Books and Articles

Barrett, Richard, and Fang Li. 1999. *Modern China.* New York: McGraw-Hill.

This small book is part of a comparative society series published by McGraw-Hill especially for sociology. The book covers

the basic social institutions in modern China, including the family, politics, and the economy. Additional chapters discuss gender issues, family planning policy, and issues of urbanization and modernization.

Chang, P. M. N. 1997. *Bound Feet and Western Dress.* Lanham, Maryland: Anchor Books.

This book is written by a first generation Chinese-American, telling the story of the women in her family in China and her remarkable aunt Chang Yu-i. Yu I is the first of her family to escape footbinding. The book describes the life of women in China as it moves into the 20th Century.

Milwertz, C. 1997. *Accepting Population Control: Urban Chinese Women and the One-Child Family Policy.* Richmond-Surrey, Curzon Press.

This book discusses the issues involved in the Chinese one-child family policy and that [policy's implications for Chinese women. The book also discusses issues involving the Chinese family and family relationships, pregnancy and childbirth and women's health in China.

Roberts, J. 1999. *A Concise History of China.* Cambridge: Harvard University Press.

This book takes the reader through 4000 years of history in 300 interesting pages. It covers all of the major Chinese dynasties into the modern era. The first half of the book takes China up to 1900, and the second half of the book is spent on the modern period.

Spence, J. 1999. *Mao Zedong.* East Rutherford, NJ: Viking Press.

One cannot understand modern China without understanding Mao Zedong and his times. This is the best short book about Mao and his enormous influence on modern China. The book covers Mao's early years and how he eventually came to lead the revolution in China. More importantly, the book shows how his utopian goals for China eventually led to the death of millions of Chinese during the Cultural Revolution.

Websites

China.Com
http://www.china.com

This site is a portal to the latest news and information sources on China.

China Education and Research Network
http://www.cernet.edu.cn/

This site is in both Chinese and English. It is a site for serious research of China and contains links to the major research institutes and organization conduction research on China.

China Today
http://www.chinatoday.com/

This site provides comprehensive information on today's China, including issues on women and children, banking, travel, ethnic issues, and economic news.

Films and Videos

Unbound voices: a documentary history of Chinese women in San Francisco, by Judy Yung. University of California (1999).

This film interviews many Chinese women living in San Francisco and chronicles their lives. These women compare their way of life in America as opposed to their former homeland, China. Differences in culture, lifestyles, and traditions become apparent as these women talk intimately about their lives.

Fanshen; a documentary of revolution in a Chinese village, by William Hinton. New York, Monthly Review Press (1967).

This film documents the social unrest in a Chinese village. Political and social issues in the village are analyzed such as land tenure, and the overall social conditions they live in are dealt with.

POLAND

BASIC DATA

Population	38,921,093
Population Growth Rate	0.05%
Per Capita GDP	$6,800
Life Expectancy at Birth	73.06 Years
Form of Government	Democratic State
Major Religions Groups	Roman Catholic 95%, Eastern Orthodox and Protestant 5%
Major Racial and Ethnic Groups	Polish 97.6%, German 1.3%, Ukrainian 0.6%
Colonial Experience	Colonized by Austria, Germany, and Russia
Principal Economic Activity	Agriculture 5.1%, Industry 26.6%, Services 68.3%

INTRODUCTION

Poland, officially the Republic of Poland, or in Polish *Rzeczpospolita Polska,* lies in the North European Plain in the area generally called Central Europe. It borders on the Baltic Sea in the north, Germany in the east, Lithuania, Belarus and Ukraine on the west, Russia on its northwest corner, and Slovakia and the Czech Republic on the southern border. The population of Poland is approximately 38 million and its land mass is slightly smaller than the state of New

Mexico. The largest city, which is also the nation's capital, is Warsaw. Ethnic Poles make up approximately 98 percent of the population of Poland, with small amounts of Germans, Ukrainians, and Byelorussia's in the border areas. At one time Poland had a large Jewish population, but most were killed in the holocaust during WWII or fled the country at that time. Most Poles are Roman Catholic and the Catholic Church plays an important role both at the national and local levels.

POLISH HISTORY

Poland has gone through three dramatic stages in the 20th Century, each of which has transformed the basic nature of Polish society: The Second World War, the domination of Poland by the Soviet Union in the post-war period, and the fall of the Iron Curtain in 1989. Poles are descendents of an ancient Slavic people known as the Polanie, referring to field or plains dwellers. The Polish people were first unified into a country in the 10th Century. After a series of foreign invasions the country was reunited under the Jagiellonian Dynasty, which lasted from the 1300's to 1572. During this period, Poland prospered and attained great heights of power and cultural achievement. This era is considered the Golden Age in Polish history. This period was followed by a series of foreign wars, invasions, occupations, and conquests that lasted essentially until the end of WWI.

At the end of WWI the Treaty of Versailles gave Poland independent status. Poland further extended its territory after a war with Russia in 1920. However, due to Germany's attack on Poland in September of 1939, an event that marked the beginning of WWII, Poland's independence was short-lived.

The Second World War was a pivotal event in Polish history. Not only did the war start in Poland, but no country experienced such immeasurable suffering than did Poland. Of a population of approximately 35 million at the beginning of 1939, over six million Poles died as a result of the war, 1.5 million in Auschwitz alone. Of the six millions Jews murdered during WWII, 3 million were Polish citizens. Other Polish casualties were the result of bombing or enslavement in concentration camps in Germany or Russia. It is estimated that twenty-two percent of the Polish population perished in WWII (Szczepanski, 1970).

At the Potsdam Conference at the end of WWII, Poland was given new boundaries and again became an independent country. Poland was located in the area of Europe under Soviet control and by 1949 a Soviet style government had come to power in Poland with close ties to the Soviet Union. Poland became part of the Eastern Bloc in the Cold War, and was cut off politically and economically from Western Europe. Poland tried several times during the decades after WWII to free itself of Soviet control. In the economic crisis of the 1970's the workers staged large demonstrations and were able to gain concessions from the government. Although the demonstrations were eventually crushed, this period saw the beginning of the Workers Solidarity Movement that was to eventually lead Poland away from Soviet rule. When the Soviet Union broke up in 1989, Poland formed a new government and Lech Welesa, the founder of the Solidarity Movement, became president.

This long history of foreign domination has had several effects on Polish society. Such lasting effects include the Polish people's aptitude for perseverance and patience in the face of seemingly insurmountable obstacles. It has also created, contrary to expectation, a strong sense of Polish national pride.

POLISH SOCIETY

Poland has historically been a country with a large peasant class. For much of its pre-modern history Poland was a feudal society, in which peasant farmers were indentured to land controlled by large landowners. Although the era of feudalism ended in the 19th Century, agricultural village life continues to inform Polish values and attitudes. Polish village life, popularized in such fictional works as **Fiddler on the Roof,** pictured a gemeinschaft society that included inflexible social roles fixed by ascribed status based on tradition and kinship. However, a closer investigation of Polish rural society shows a more complex status system with numerous levels, continuous competition between individuals and families for village honor and status, and some amount of social mobility.

In Polish society the family and church play significant roles. Family members are expected to help each other, and extended kinship ties remain strong. In the bureaucratic society during the rule of the Communist Party, connections through family contacts or friendships, called *dojscie,* were used in the informal sector of society to gain access to certain areas of the bureaucracy that were formally off-limits.

THE CATHOLIC CHURCH

The Catholic Church has played a long and important role in Polish society. The Church is not just a religious institution, but also a political and social force, and an integral part of the Polish nationality. The Catholic Church is so important in Poland that Church activities and influence continued unabated during Communist rule. Ninety-six percent of Poles are Catholics and the Church dominates their lives from birth to death. They are baptized in the Church, married in the Church, and buried in the Church. An example of the power of the Catholic Church in Polish society is the issue of a woman's right to an abortion. Although the majority of Poles favor abortion rights, the Catholic Church insisted that abortions be made illegal in Poland.

Some scholars have suggested that the strength of the Catholic Church in Poland is in part because of its focus on the Virgin Mary and the Christian Saints, rather than on the direct relationship between the individual and God. The most important religious pilgrimage in Poland is the image of the Virgin, called the Black Madonna, at Jasna Gora Monastery in Czestochowa. The image is believed to have rescued the Polish nation from the invasion of the Tatars and the Swedes, and Polish leaders commonly wear replicas of the icon. In this imagery, the Virgin Mary comes to stand for the Polish nation and her suffering is the suffering of Poland.

RACIAL AND ETHNIC GROUPS

Poland is now a monoethnic society, but during most of its history it has been multiethnic. Before the war there were large populations of Jews, Germans, Ukrainians, Belarusians, and Gypsies. The largest, and most influential, ethnic group in Poland was the Jews. Before the WWII, there were about 3 million Jews in Poland, which comprised not only ten percent of the Polish population, but were also the largest Jewish community in Europe. They were an active and important part of Polish life and lived in both rural and urban areas. Most were killed in the Holocaust, many in death camps in Poland itself. Of the 200,000 or so who survived the war, almost all fled Poland for other places, notably Israel or the United States. There are now only about 10,000 Jews in Poland, most of whom are elderly.

There is some debate regarding the level of Polish anti-Semitism that existed before the War and to what extent it still exists today. Before the war Jewish and non-Jewish Poles had lived together for centuries, albeit in separate villages or neighborhoods. Yet anti-Jewish prejudice and discrimination did exist in Poland before the war. Jews were often scapegoated and blamed for problems in Poland, and the Poles resented the fact that the Jewish communities spoke Yiddish rather than Polish. On the other hand, the fiercest anti-Semites were the Nazis in Germany, and the Holocaust was planned and executed by the Germans.

More disturbing has been the increase in anti-Semitism in the post cold war era, which some have called "anti-Semitism without Jews." For instance, in the elections of 1990 Polish candidates traded charges of being under Jewish influence, even though there is no Jewish community left in Poland, forcing Lech Welesa to apologize to Israel for remarks made by some of the political candidates. In a survey conducted in Poland in 1992, 40 percent of the Poles thought that the Jewish population was about 75,000 (it is only about 10,000), and 26 percent thought that the Jews still exerted too much influence in Polish society.

Germans, White Russians, and Ukrainians also constituted a large part of the Polish population before WWII. The Germans and the Poles have had a long and troublesome relationship. Although the Poles continue to fear the Germans, now more for their economic prowess than their military might, many Poles are proud to claim German ancestry, especially in the southern area of Silesia where the local dialect is a mixture of Polish and German. Before the war, ethnic Germans constituted perhaps as many as 2 million in Poland, but most left Poland during or after the war. In addition, the Polish/German border was redrawn after WWII to exclude some of the ethnic Germans. There were also about 1.5 million Ukrainians in Poland who either fled to the Soviet Union after WWII or were expelled.

Gypsies, called *Rom* in Central Europe, make up a small part of the Polish population, numbering at the most 50,000. The Gypsies constitute a much larger segment of the population of Romania and the Czech Republic where their presence is more controversial. Though Gypsies are considered a problem in Central and Western Europe and several countries have a "Gypsy Policy" to control their movement and actions, Poland has no official Gypsy policy. Despite the absence of a "Gypsy Policy" Gypsies are still discriminated against in Poland, as in much of Europe. For instance, they are blamed for crimes, especially prostitution, theft, and fraud, and for violent acts that may or may not be of their doing.

SOCIAL STRATIFICATION

The Polish class system looks somewhat different than the class system of Western European countries or the United States. The strong role of the intelligentsia, the devastation of the middle class during WWII, and the creation of a bureaucratic upper class under socialist rule characterize the Polish stratification system. Though there are intelligent and learned people in the United States, they do not, however, form a social class nor play such an important role in society as does the intelligentsia in Eastern and Central European countries. Not only has the Polish intelligentsia played an important role in Polish history, but also it continues to play an important role in Poland. For instance, the intellegentsia are the chief repositories of polish society and culture, and the innovator of new ideas and social inventions. Recognized as a separate class in Poland, many of the intelligentsia occupy high positions in government agencies, political parties, and as writers and academics.

Poland also has a strong working class. The Polish working class can be divided into agricultural workers and the urban industrial workers. Once the largest and most important class in Poland, the agricultural workers are now leaving the farms in record numbers and migrating to the cities to work in industries that pay better. In the agricultural villages, the unemployment rate remains high and many small family farms are going under. Today, industry plays a larger role in the Polish economy, and accounts for 30 percent of the labor force, compared to 26 percent in the agricultural sector.

Poland is now experiencing considerable upward social mobility. The rapid growth in the Polish economy and the shortage of skilled workers is creating opportunities for lower class workers to move up in society. However, the key to upward mobility in modern Polish society is education, since much of the work in the new economic sector is in high technology companies.

THE ROLE OF WOMEN

Women have played a dominant role in Polish history and society, but mostly in the domestic sphere. In traditional Polish culture, the Polish woman is seen as strong, maternal, religious, and with many children. This traditional woman's role has been immortalized in Polish poems and songs. However, under the Communist government the educational and occupational opportunities for women expanded, surpassing even those of Western Europe. By the mid-1970's, nearly half of all Polish women were in the work force, and women had made gains in traditional male occupations such as engineering and medicine. Women have also advanced in the agricultural sector, where women presently run about 20 percent of the farms. This, however, is often out of economic necessity since in many cases the men have left the farm to work in the cities, leaving the farms to the women.

In education, Polish women have also made great strides. Between 1975 and 1985 the number of women in higher education more than doubled, and in some areas, such as medical school, women now make up over 60 percent of the students. At the present time, female enrollment in school equals or exceeds male enrollment. In secondary school, females out number males by 5 percent. More importantly, 31 percent of Polish women in higher education are focusing on science subjects, one of the highest percentages in Europe.

In government, women have also made strides. Poland selected a woman prime minister in 1992, Hanna Suchocka, and a woman was named to the very important position as head of the National Bank of Poland. The only institution where women have still not made inroads into higher positions is in the Catholic Church.

Despite these successes, the advances of women in public life have come at a price. Polish society, especially the Catholic Church, continues to stress women's role in the home as mother and homemaker. For instance, studies found that Polish women who worked full time also spent on average 4.3 hours per day doing housework. And although birthrates have fallen dramatically in Poland and 75 percent of couples report using birth control, the Catholic Church continues to deny women reproductive control.

POPULATION TRENDS

Poland currently has a population of approximately 39 million people. Poland's population is not expected to grow much in the future and is predicted to remain at about the same size in 2015. After that point the population will begin to decline. This low population growth and future decline is largely related to Poland's very low fertility rate. **The total fertility rate**, which measures how many children a woman will have over her lifetime at present fertility levels, is 1.45, one of the lowest in the world. This means that the average Polish family is having 1.45 children, clearly below replacement level, which requires about 2 children per family

Like other countries with a low birthrate Poland is facing a critical shortage of workers. Unlike some of the other European counties such as Germany, which import a large number of foreign workers each year, Poland has not experienced the importation of foreign workers. In fact, Poland continues to experience a net out migration, with more people leaving than arriving. This out migration coupled with the low birthrate has created critical labor shortages in some industries. Although Poland is one of the economic bright spots in Central Europe, wages and economic opportunities still lag behind the wages and opportunities in Western Europe and the United States. Poles, therefore, still look to immigrate to Western Europe or the United States, although this flow has slowed greatly in the last decade.

In 1999 Poland's crude death rate, the number of people of all ages that die per 1000 people, was 9.72 deaths per 1000 population. The average life expectancy for Polish women is 77 years and a for men, 69 years. Poland also has an infant mortality rate of 12.76 deaths for every 1000 children born in the first year of life. These statistics indicate that Polish society is relatively healthy, although a bit behind the standards of Western Europe.

ECONOMICS

The Polish economy is doing better than most of the economies of Eastern and Central Europe countries, that is, of those countries making the transition from a command economy to a free market economy. The transition to a market economy is proving difficult for many countries that were formerly in the Eastern Bloc, and many of these countries, including Russia itself, have seen both dramatic falls in economic output and in standards of living in the decade after Communism. After the fall of the Communist government, Poland was quick to liberalize its markets and to privatize the state industries, something many former East block countries have still not done. In addition, the Polish workforce is well educated and wages remain low. As a result, after 1990 there has been a rapid growth of new business ventures. The annual growth rate of GDP in 1998 is estimated to be 5.6 percent. Also encouraging economic growth is a very low national dept, calculated as less than 2 percent of GDP. Living standards have also increased; the per capita GDP, a measure of the countries total economic output per person, was almost $7,000 in 1999, one of the highest in Central Europe.

On the other hand, the Polish economy has some rough spots. For one, agriculture lags behind the rest of the economy. Twenty-eight percent of the working Poles are employed in agriculture, but they produce only 6.5 percent of the nations economic output. In addition, farming continue to be inefficient, using out-dated technology on farm plots that are too small to be economic. This has forced farmers to flee the countryside for the city.

The Polish economy will soon be facing a major test as it prepares to join the European Union. Poland is eager to join the EU, but to do so it will have to make a number of economic changes, including opening its borders to European business and workers, including German businesses. EU membership will also require Poland to implement stronger environmental standards. Many of Poland's industries are heavy polluters and Polish water and air is among the dirtiest in Europe.

MODERNIZATION

Like many countries that are developing rapidly, modernization in Poland is uneven. In many of the larger cities, particularly Warsaw, all the conveniences and annoyances of modern life are present. On the other hand, in some of the rural villages, Polish life resembles that of centuries past. Yet Poland clearly yearns to be part of modern Europe after centuries of isolation and foreign domination, and now that the Iron Curtain has fallen. Poland is moving rapidly to become a modern country. Poland leads the other countries in Central Europe in the percentage of the population with telephones, computers, and television. In addition, Poland is becoming a tourist destination, which increases its exposure to the world. Poland has recently been accepted into NATO, bringing it closer to Western Europe and the United States. Poles desire a modern life, with more conveniences and a higher standard of living.

On the other hand, Poles are naturally cautious regarding the outside world. Their history of invasions and foreign rule reminds them to be cautious. Poland is particularly concerned about its neighbor Germany. On the one hand, Poland envies Germany's economic and industrial success. On the other hand, Poland fears that their membership into the European Common Market will open its borders to German firms and German agriculture who will look to take advantage of Poland's inexpensive land prices and cheap labor.

SUMMARY

Poland is a country of approximately 38 million people in the northern part of Central Europe. Poland has had a long history of foreign invasion and domination and has been ruled by the Germans, Austrians, and the Russians to name a few. Poland suffered greatly during WWII when over six million Poles were killed; three million of whom were Jews. Poland was once a multiethnic society, but modern Poland is composed mostly of ethnic Poles. Anti-Semitic views still exist in Poland. The Catholic Church plays a strong role in Polish society, both at the national and local level. The Polish intelligentsia form a distinct social class in Poland and play a major role in Polish society. Population growth has flattened due to Poland's very low birth rate, and the population can be expect to begin to decrease in the future. This will in turn create a shortage of skilled labor. Poland's economy has done well after the fall of the Iron Curtain, and it is making a smooth transition to a market economic system.

Poles are open to modernization and seek the life style of Western Europe and the United States. Poland has joined NATO and is seeking to join the European Union.

READINGS

Introduction

This article, "Poland's Second City: Upheaval" which appeared in the **Economist** in October of 1999, describes some of the major obstacles facing Poland's attempt to transform itself from a socialist country to a modern country with a market driven economy. It focuses on the industrial city of Lodz, Poland's second largest city. Lodz was once a prosperous city, the "Polish Manchester, referring to its leadership in industrial production and had a large and prosperous Jewish community before the War. Now the old state-run industries cannot compete on the world market, and the standard of living has fallen. However, young western oriented businessmen are developing new high tech service industries that may lead Lodz into a new prosperous era.

Reading

"Poland's Second City: Upheaval." *Economist*. October 23, 1999, pp. 56–57.

Study Questions

1. This article points out some of the major difficulties Poland is facing as it makes the transformation from a socialist country to a capitalist country. What are the major obstacles that Poland is facing in this transition? How are these obstacles related to Poland's historical past?

2. The article reports that Lodz has 16 percent more females than males, and that women say they have a hard time finding a husband. What do you think has caused this female imbalance? Where are the males?

POLAND'S SECOND CITY: UPHEAVAL

It is a cold, grey autumn morning ten years after the collapse of communism. A lorry is delivering a winter's supply of coal to a re- tired widower in a poor district of Lodz (pronounced Woodge), Poland's second city. The widower stands outside her tiny terraced house, arms folded, glowering fiercely. The coal costs too much, she moans. "Life was much better before 1989" Work was easier, and she had a free holiday at the seaside every summer. Coal was free too, she adds.

The coalmen, three of them, steam in the frigid air from all the shovelling and carrying. "She's right about one thing," one of them says. "Life was much easier ten years ago." He leans on his shovel and wipes his blackened brow. "There's not much in the new Poland for people like me and her." Like you? "You know," he says bitterly, "the old, the thick, the working man."

To make a living, the men drive their decrepit Soviet-era lorry through the night, selling coal by the bucket. They cannot under-stand why life is so hard for them, while others, especially young people, seem to have it easy. "It's like magic," says one. "We're struggling just to survive and all these kids have money to spend on music and clothes."

For sure, in the past decade the economy of Lodz has been turned on its head. Almost every aspect of life has been touched by communism's fall—and Poland's return to the West. In 1821, Lodz had only 800 inhabitants; within 50 years, the industrial revolution had made it the "Polish Manchester", a smoky textile city that supplied Russia with most of its cloth. For the Germans, Poles and Jews who made their fortunes here, Lodz was the promised land depicted in Andrzej Wajda's epic film of the same name. Jews in particular flourished until their Lodz community, one of the largest in Europe, was wiped out in the Holocaust.

For all its grime, Lodz always had a strong cultural life too. Here, in 1932, French and Polish avante-garde artists set up one of Europe's first galleries of modern art. Architects experimented as well. The city is still home to the Polish Film School, where directors such as Roman Polanski studied.

The titanic red-brick mill built by Izrael Poznanski, Lodz's most flamboyant industrialist, still stands sentinel over the heart of the city, a cathedral to 19th-century capitalism. In 1989, 12,500 people worked in it. Now it is hauntingly deserted. The vast ornate iron gates that workers once poured through are padlocked. A small Solidarity office that served the workers is boarded up, its hand-painted sign flaking. A lone security guard sits in a poky office by the gate watching a game-show on a black and white television. "I heard some French people are going to turn the place into a hotel and leisure centre," he says. "My granny used to work here, you know. Everyone's granny worked here."

In 1989, 90% of Lodz's people were in textiles and fibres, mostly destined for the Soviet Union. But when Poland entered the free market, the mills were destroyed by rivals in the Far East Trade with Russia collapsed. Almost all Lodz's state enterprises went bust. Now little more than half of the city's economy still runs on textiles; state-owned companies produce only 5% of Lodzs output.

Instead, a roaring new service industry has created thousands of jobs. At the last count, Lodz had 71,000 small businesses, employing 85% of the city's workers. Some new outfits draw on the city's tradition of tailoring, winning contracts to make clothes for companies with smart names like Pierre Cardin. Others have gone a step further, setting up their own clothing firms. Hypermarkets have sprouted in the husks of Lodz's abandoned factories.

Still, this revolution has been painful. More than 11% of people in Lodz have no job. Women say it is hard to get a husband—in a city with 16% more females than males; and more than a fifth of the women are on the dole. Lodz's population, now 810,000, has been shrinking.

But the pain is beginning to have good results. The ill-educated and unskilled are worst hit, but even they have more possessions these days. Across the social spectrum, ownership of cars and homes has soared. The nostalgists tend to forget that in 1989 you had to queue for bread; now you can choose between croissants and bagels. "Communists built big buildings with small flats," says a builder. "Now we're building small buildings with big flats."

Besides, as Adam Michnik, once a dissident, now a leading editor in Warsaw, points out, the ideal society people dreamed of in 1989 was bound to be, unattainable. "Poles wanted the shopping and nightlife of Manhattan, the security of the Swedish welfare state and the work habits of communism," he says. "That wasn't a real choice."

RESOURCES FOR FURTHER STUDY

Books and Articles

Cordell, Karl ed. 2000. *Poland and the European Union*. Florence, KY: Routledge Press.

> *This book discusses Poland's relationship with the European Union and its attempt to join the Union. This book covers Poland's contemporary politics and the politics of Eastern Europe in general, as well as the role of the government and the economy in modern Poland. Poland's relationship with Western Europe is also discussed.*

Davies, Norman. 1986. *Heart of Europe: A Short History of Poland*. New York: Oxford University Press.

> *This book gives a readable account of Polish history. It covers both the beginning of the Polish people in the 10th Century, but also the modern period of Polish history during and after WWII. It does not, unfortunately, cover the period after the fall of the Iron Curtain. The book also argues that the Poles should not be held responsible for the plight of the Jews during WWII, since they themselves were captives and in need of help.*

Nomberg-Prsuytyk, Sara and Roslyn Hirsch. 1986. *Auschwitz: True Tales from a Grotesque Land*. Chapel Hill: University of North Carolina Press.

> *This book describes the holocaust that took place in Auschwitz, Poland. Although the Germans were the major executioners of the holocaust, most of the Jews who were killed were non-German Jews, and the largest group of Jews executed was from Poland.*

Thomas, William I., and Florian Znaniecki. 1958. *The Polish Peasant in Europe and America*. Champaign: University of Illinois.

> *This classic work on the Polish peasant has been edited by Eli Zaretsky and re-released. Although the study was done in the early part of the 20th Century it still readable and tells us much about the life of the Polish peasant and the process of assimilation in the United States. The work was done during the period when many immigrants were coming to America to seek a better life, not just the Poles.*

Websites

Poland Home Page
http://poland.pl/

> *This is the main homepage for Poland. It includes information on Polish society,*

the Polish State, culture and the arts, science and education, and the economy.

Inside Poland

http://www.insidepoland.pl/

This website has information about Poland, including current news, economic information, and travel.

Films and Videos

The Jews in Polish culture, by Lucjan Dobroszycki. Evanston, IL: Northwestern University Press (1988).

This film focuses on the Jewish population in Poland and the anti-Semitism and

Polish World-Internet Guide to Poland and Polonia

http://www.polishworld.com/

This website has generally information about Poland. It is largely a travel guide, but it also has useful information for the researcher.

prejudice that is and was a part of Polish society. In addition, one will get a overall sense of ethnic relations in Poland.

IRAN

BASIC DATA

Population	65,179,7522
Population Growth Rate	1.07%
Per Capita GDP	$5,000
Life Expectancy at Birth	69.76 Years
Form of Government	Theocratic Republic
Major Religions	Shi'a Islam 89%, Sunni Islam 10%, Zoroastrian, Jewish, Christian, and Baha'i 1%
Major Racial and Ethnic Groups	Persian 51%, Azerbaijani 24%, Kurds 7%
Colonial Experience	None
Principal Economic Activity	Petroleum and petrochemicals, textiles

INTRODUCTION

Iran, officially the Islamic Republic of Iran, or in Persian, *Jomhuri-e Islami-e Iran,* is a country in the region of the world called the Middle East. It has a population of over 65 million, and borders on the Persian Gulf in the south, Afghanistan and Pakistan in the east, Turkmenistan, Azerbaijan and Armenia in the north, and Turkey and Iraq in the west. The country has sometimes been called Persia in the western world, the Greek word, but the Iranians have always preferred to call their country Iran. Persian refers to the language and culture of the country.

Iranians are different than the other peoples of the Middle East in that they are not Semitic, as are the Arabs and the Hebrews, nor are they Turkic, as are the Turks and the Azerbaijanis. Rather the Iranians are of Indo-European descent, as are most Europeans. The language of Iran, Persian, is an Indo-European language, and although it contains many Arabic and Turkish loan words, it is closer in syntax and structure to German or English, than to Arab or Turkish. The word "Iran" is linguistically the same word as "Aryan", and the Iranians are aware of the fact that they are descendents of the Aryans, another term for Indo-European. Mohammed Reza Shah Pahlavi, the last Shah of Iran, gave himself the title of *Arya-Mehr,* or light of the Aryans to emphasize Iran's Aryan roots.

Although ethnic Persians comprise approximately 51 percent of the Iranian population and thus are the largest proportion of the population, there are other ethnic-linguistic groups in the country as well. These include Azerbaijanis, who make up about 24 percent of the population, and smaller populations of Kurds, Arabs, and other groups. The Persian language is the official language of Iran, and the language of instruction at all schools and for all newspapers. However, a sizeable minority of Iranians speaks other languages, including Turkic languages and Arabic. Many Iranians are bilingual or even trilingual. Most Iranians are Moslems of the Shi'a branch (most Moslems in the World are of the Sunni branch), but small indigenous communities of Jews, Christians, Zoroastrians, and Baha'is also live in Iran.

IRANIAN SOCIAL STRUCTURE

Iran has been until recently an agricultural and pastoral society. As a result, the Iranian social structure has its roots in the traditional rural societies. The settled agriculturalists, largely subsistence farmers, were organized in a form of feudalism in which the landlords lived in the major cities rather than on their respective farms. This type of absentee feudalism is common in parts of Asia and different from the estate feudalism that existed in Europe. In the traditional rural Iranian social system there are two levels; the landlords and the peasants, and the gulf between them was profound and great.

Iran also is the home to nomadic pastoralists organized into patronymic tribes. While pastoral nomads make a small percent of the current Iranian population, they may have constituted as much as 50% of the population in 1900. Tribal structures have two characteristics; they have an ethos of equalitarianism among male adult tribal members, and they are strongly patriarchal. The Iranian tribes have played a dominant role in Iranian history. Most of the shahs, or kings, of Iran have descended from tribes.

The urban social structure has been a dominant feature of Iranian social life as well. The social elite has always lived in the cities, and the cities are the hub of Iranian social, economic, and political life. Iran has several regional capitals, although the capital city, Tehran, now dominates Iran. Tehran is also a new city. Some of the regional cities such as Isfahan, Shiraz, and Mashad have ancient pasts.

STRATIFICATION AND INEQUALITY

Iran is organized into three social classes. The upper class is composed of two groups, the high-level Islamic clergy, and wealthy businessmen who support the clergy. These two segments of the upper class work closely together, since successful businesses need the blessing of the clergy to survive, and the clergy, in turn, need the financial support of the businessmen. The upper class of the 1960's and 1970's made up mostly of rich capitalists and members of the royal family fled Iran after the revolution in 1979.

The middle class is composed of several groups as well: the educated professionals, such as teachers, medical doctors, engineers, etc; middle ranking clergy who hold many of the important bureaucratic positions in the Iranian government; and the small shopkeepers and traders that constitute the bazaar. These groups have been in conflict since the Iranian revolution of 1979, since members of the first group, which might be called the modern middle class, typically have western educations and a more secular orientation than the clergy or the bazaarkeepers. Many members of the modern middle class desire a more modern lifestyles, free from Islamic constraints and are the major supporters of liberalization. On the other hand, the clergy and bazaarkeepers form an interlocking conservative partnership supporting the religious injunctions.

The Iranian lower class is also composed of several groups. The industrial workers in Iran's factories, services, and mills constitute a new working class, although they have yet to develop working class awareness or solidarity. Most of these industries suffered after the Islamic Revolution in 1979, and the living conditions of the industrial workers have fallen.

There are also a large number of underemployed or unemployed people in Iran. Many of them are farmers who have been forced off of their land by land reform or poor farming conditions, and have moved to the cities to find work. They survive by begging or selling small items on the street. This group of unemployed has become a major problem in the larger cities, particularly Tehran.

FAMILY

The traditional Iranian family is patriarchal (the men have the power), patrilineal (inheritance through the male side), and patrilocal (the bride moves into the husbands household at the time of marriage). The man is responsible for the safety and welfare of the family and the woman's responsibility is to bear children and to provide the domestic support. The traditional Iranian family live in extended households and the children live at home until marriage. The typical Iranian extended household lives in a dwelling that features a courtyard surrounded by a high wall, with rooms around the parameter and an open area, often with a pool, in the center. Often several brothers with their nuclear families live in the same compound with the older parents. In the compound, older children attend to younger children, the grandparents socialize the children, and women perform the domestic chores. However, in modern Iranian cities, this traditional lifestyle is disappearing as urban crowding is forcing Iranian families to move into apartments where it is difficult for extended families to live together.

In Iran, as in much of the Middle East, marriages are viewed as important to the entire family, and are therefore usually arranged by the parents. Even in modern Iranian marriages, the parents are consulted and the pretense of an arranged marriage is still maintained. Among the villagers in the rural areas of Iran, women are married at a young age, often before fifteen.

GENDER

There is much misunderstanding and misinformation about gender roles in Iran. While the west pictures Iranian women in veils living secluded lives, women in Iran play a greater role in society than do women in most other Moslem countries. The role of women in Iranian society is based on two principles. The first deals with the role of the woman in the household and the family, and her relation to men, referred to as patriarchy. In a patriarchal society such as Iran, a woman's role is in the household as a mother, a daughter, or a wife. A women's status in the larger society is determined by her relationship to men. A women is born a man's daughter and maybe a brother's sister, she later becomes a different man's wife, and finally, if she is lucky, a mother to a son. At all stages of her life, she is defined by the males in her life and her relationship to them.

The second principle that determines a women's role in Iranian society involves a women's sexuality and is defined by behaviors of modesty and virtue. Female modesty has three components: Virginity before marriage; fidelity during marriage; and appropriate behavior in public. Codes of appropriate public behavior involve rules of proper dress, public segregation of the sexes, and the avoidance of any flirtatious behaviors, including eye contact with males.

These rules of modesty mainly apply to women in the public domain; the private lives of women are another matter. Since traditional Iranian households often have a high wall surrounding the courtyard, women are not required to be veiled or to follow other restrictive behavior while at home.

Women in Iran, however, are not restricted only to the home and are allowed to go to school and enter occupations that are thought suitable. For instance, 48 percent of the medical students in Iran are women, and many women go into teaching. Iran is also one of the few Islamic countries that have women elected to parliament. In addition, one of the vice presidents in the present government is a woman.

GOVERNMENT

In 1979 Iran witnessed a revolution that saw the Shah of Iran, who had ruled for 37 years, overthrown and Islamic government put in its place. While the form of this new Islamic government appeared to be a return to an older form of rule, in fact it was a new creation. In fact, the new Islamic Constitutions was modeled on the French parliamentary form of government. The core of the federal government is an elected parliament and a separately elected president. To ensure that the government adheres to Islamic principles, there is also an independent branch of Islamic overseers that can override or veto any of the decisions of the parliament or the president. This Islamic branch has two parts; the position of Supreme Islamic Leader, which is appointed for life, and the Council of Guardians, composed of six Islamic jurists and six lay judges. This governmental form was constructed to combine the principles of a democratic parliamentarian government, with the principles of a government of Islamic law. Despite many problems, a massive war with Iraq, the assassination of several leaders, the bombing of the prime ministers office, and the ostracisms of the world community, this government has survived for over twenty years.

POPULATION ISSUES

Iran is one of the most populace countries in the Middle East at approximately 65 million. In the last few years, the Iranian birthrate has fallen dramatically. In 1986 the total fertility rate, which measures how many live births a women will have at current birthrates, was 7.0 children per woman. By 1999 the total fertility rate was down to 2.45 children per woman. However, despite the drop in the fertility rate, the Iranian population is still growing fast and this population increase is creating problems for Iran. For one, a high birthrate means that there is a high ratio of children to working adults in the population. Thirty-six percent of the Iranian population is under the age of sixteen years old.

In addition to the decrease in the fertility rate in Iran, the mortality rate has also decreased. The infant mortality rate, the measure of how many children die in the first year of life for every 1000 born, is estimated to be about 20 per 1000 births in 1999, down from 133 in 1970. For comparisons, the United States infant mortality rate in 1999 was 7 deaths per 1000 born. In addition, the average life expectancy from birth has risen in Iran to 68 years for males and 71 years for females.

URBANIZATION

While today's Iranian cities play an important role in Iran, until the 1980's over fifty percent of the population still lived in the rural areas. However, rapid urbanization is now occurring in Iran so that over sixty percent of the population live in the urban areas. This rapid urbanization has created problems of overcrowding in all of the major cities, but the problems caused by overurbanization are particularly acute in Tehran, where population growth has outstripped the city's ability to provide services such as sanitation, schools, and clean water. The population in Tehran, a relatively new city by Iranian standards, went from one million in the 1950's to over 12 million today. It has become one of the most crowded cities in the world, with enormous satellite-cities of poor people surrounding the city. One out of ever five Iranians now lives in Tehran or in one of its suburbs.

Many of the people moving to Tehran are farmers who have been forced off of their land. As is common in third world cities, the poor live in shanty-towns on the outskirts of the city, forming huge satellite cities, each with populations of hundreds of thousands of people. This large and growing poor urban population strains municipal services and creates the possibility for social unrest.

RELIGION

Approximately 90 percent of Iranians are Moslems of the Shi'a branch. Shi'a Islam forms a separate branch of Islam and differs from Sunni Islam (which makes up the majority of Islam) over interpretations of who are the proper descendents of the Prophet Mohammed. Although there are Shi'a in other Islamic countries, Iran is the only country where Shi'a Islam is the officialreligion. In Iran, religious scholars called *Mujtahids* carry a great deal of status and power, and are able to interpret Islamic law. Among the *Mujtahids* are several levels, the highest being an *Ayatollah,* literally "sign of god". The *Ayatollah* is not a priest, but is rather an Islamic scholar and jurist. Most *Ayatollahs* are leaders of Islamic seminaries, *madrasehs,* and have large followings. The *Mujtahids* now hold the major governmental roles in the Iranian government.

Islam holds that a good Moslem should obey the five pillars of Islam. These prescribed actions include stating your belief in god, prayer, tithing, fasting, and pilgrimage. Iranians also place particular emphasis on the descendents of the Prophet Mohammed through the line of Ali, one of the original Caliphs, or followers of the Prophet Mohammed. Iranian iconology has taken the persecution of Ali and his descendents as a metaphor for the persecution of Iran itself, turning Shi'ism from a religious belief to a revolutionary ideology.

After the Islamic revolution in 1979, Islamic rules have been applied to most spheres of life in Iran. Many Iranians accept living under the strict Islamic rule, but some Iranians do not. The Iranians who do not want to follow the rules of Islam have either fled Iran or found ways to accommodate to the Islamic edicts in their everyday lives.

ECONOMY

The Iranian economy suffers from too much of a good thing, oil. Iran has some of the world's largest oil reserves and obtains much of its foreign currency from petroleum exports. However, the over-dependence on petroleum puts Iran's economic fortunes at the whims of the world oil prices, and has kept the Iranian economy from diversifying. In the early 1990's when oil prices fell Iran experienced an economic crisis and was forced to reschedule over 15 billion dollars in international loans. However, the increase in oil prices in 1996 helped Iran survive the financial crisis. In addition, the United State's sanctions on business with Iran have hurt economic development.

The Iranian economy continues to struggle and the standard of living, as measured by per capita GDP, has actually fallen over the last decade. The per capita GDP was estimated to be approximately $5,000 in 1998. Statistics also show that about 30 percent of the Iranian workforce is unemployed, and that 53 percent of the population lives below the poverty line. In addition, Iran continues to experience a shortage of skilled labor in many of its industries.

Iranian agriculture is also not doing well. Only about 10 percent of the land of Iran is suitable for farming, the rest being desert or mountains. Yet this 10 percent of land, if efficiently farmed, could adequately feed the whole Iranian population. However, Iran continues to import much of its food.

MODERNIZATION

Since the revolution in 1979, Iran has sought to isolate itself from the western world, especially those aspects of western society that were seen as decadent and against the teaching of Islam. The United States was identified as the "Great Satan" in Iran (the former Soviet Union was called the "Lesser Satan".) As a result, such things as western music, some aspects of western dress, and western television and movies were been banned in Iran. However, the Iranian leaders make a distinction between the good and bad parts of western culture. As a result, Iran has remained open to western technology and science, as well as western scholarship in the humanities and social sciences.

Though Iran is often times closed off to the rest of the world, Iran is none-theless not immune from the forces of globalization. Since more and more Iranians are traveling and since international tourism to Iran is beginning to pick up, exposure to western influences is increasing. In addition, such things a the Internet, satellite dishes, and smuggled videotapes and CD's, while illegal in Iran, are difficult to detect and control. As a result, western influences are readily evident in modern Iran.

There is now a growing demand in Iran for a more open society that would allow more tolerant attitudes towards women, a relaxation of strict Islamic codes of behavior and dress, a greater freedom for the press, and the acceptance of different lifestyles. The election of President Khatami in 1998 was seen as a step in this direction. He has been slowly modernizing and liberalizing Iran. He has even made tentative approaches towards the Great Satan.

IRAN'S FUTURE

Iran experienced a revolution in 1979 that ranks among the greatest revolutions of all time. Millions of Iranians from all walks of life took to the streets in the cities and towns of Iran to throw out Mohammed Reza Shah Pahlavi, and his cronies and supporters. There anger was also directed at the United States, who the demonstrators felt had aided and abetted the Shah's rule. Mohammed Reza had ruled Iran for 37 years and was the last of a 2500-year reign of powerful monarchs. As with all major revolutions, Iranian society was turned upside down, and Iran turned to the Shi'a Islamic clergy to build a new Iran based on Islamic ideals and principles. What might appear to the western eyes to be a new harsh regime was in fact a natural purging of old ways and the attempt to find a new path for Iran.

But the revolution is now over twenty years old. Over fifty percent of the Iranian population were born after the revolution and therefore have no direct experience of the period of the Shah or of the revolution itself. This new generation wants a better life, jobs, more freedoms, and access to modern culture. They no longer want to live under the harsh rules of Islamic codes. This is the new Iran. This is the Iran that voted in President Khatami, and this is the Iran that will determine the future.

SUMMARY

Iran is one of the largest countries in the Middle East with a population of over 65 million. Although in the Middle East, Iranians are actually descendents of the early Indo-Europeans. Ethnic Persians make a majority of Iranians, but other ethno-linguistic groups live in Iran as well, including Azerbaijanis, Kurds, and Arabs. Iranians have a strong family system that emphasizes patriarchal values and extended families. Women are expected to follow the dictates of Islam and remain subservient to the males in her life, but women have also achieved educational and occupational advancements in modern Iran. Most Iranians are Shi'a Moslems. The Shi'a clergy now control the government of Iran and Islamic laws control much of Iranian life. Iran is experiencing rapid urbanization that is bringing crowding to the major cities. Over twenty years after its major revolution that overthrew Mohammed Reza Shah, Iran is beginning to open up to the rest of the world and beginning the process of modernization.

READING

Introduction

The following article, *Iranian Women Seek Equality*, reveals the changing roles of women in Iranian society. While Islamic law, which plays a central role in Iranian society, not only places women under the rule and supervision of men, it has also placed restrictions on women in all areas of life, restrictions which are not placed upon men. These restrictions have essentially curtailed and limited women's freedom and roles in Iranian society. Today, Iranian women are defying these "restrictions" in record numbers, and are becoming more visible in all areas of society, even government, which has always been a powerful symbol of male privilege and authority.

Reading

Iranian Women Seek Equality, by BBC News.

Study Questions

1. Like all societal institutions, religion and religious interpretation, is unstable and is always changing. How then are Iranian women interconnected with Islam and their roles in society?
2. How do you think a woman's larger and more visible roles in Iranian society will impact Iran's future? Do you think women's higher status in Iran could have a global impact? If so, how?

IRANIAN WOMEN SEEK EQUALITY

Three years ago, women voted in their millions for reformist President Mohammad Khatami. He in turn is now encouraging them to play a bigger role in politics.

A record 513 women stood in the 18 February polls. They made up about 7% of candidates nationwide, and nearly 15% in the capital Tehran.

"Until now, women's rights and sensitivities were derided in Iran and it is our role and our obligation to restore these rights," says one candidate, Vahideh Talaqani.

She is one of several women members of the pro-Khatami Islamic Iran Participation Front who are campaigning for equal pay and the abolition of forced marriages.

The restrictions imposed on women in Iran are less severe than in some of the Gulf Arab states, which bar women even from driving.

But the Islamic law in force since the 1979 revolution places women under male supervision and requires them to follow a strict dress code.

Over the past 20 years, the Iranian clergy have stressed the traditional family role of women and the majority of conservative clerics still believe men are superior to women.

This is evident in a number of religious and civil laws, which many women candidates are seeking to change.

For example, the value of a woman's life in Iran is half that of a man's in terms of blood money, and her testimony in court is also worth half that of a man.

A woman is rarely granted custody of children unless they are very young. And, if her husband dies, his father gains authority over the couple's assets.

'Bad Treatment'

But President Khatami has said that, according to Islam, there is no difference between men and women.

And last year a senior cleric, Ayatollah Yosef Sanei, made headlines when he declared there should be nothing to stop a woman becoming president or even supreme religious leader—a post generally believed to be ordained by God.

Ayatollah Sanei said women's "bad treatment" since the Islamic Revolution contradicted the teachings of Islam.

And he said it was wrong not to allow women to become judges or to accept them as full witnesses in courts.

There were women judges before the revolution, but they were removed in 1979. In recent years they have been brought back, but so far only in an advisory capacity.

However, many commentators say women have made significant gains since the revolution, compared with life under the shahs.

Iranian women are generally well educated and more women now attend university than men.

They are gradually moving into male work spheres, such as the police force, and they have entered the government.

One of Iran's vice-presidents, Masoumeh Ebtekar, is a woman, and women held 14 of the 270 parliamentary seats before the general election.

Women candidates also did well in last year's local polls—the first since the revolution—winning the highest number of votes in 109 cities.

As in 1979, when they were in the vanguard of the street protests that toppled the Shah, Iran's women are once again playing a dominant role in the movement for change.

RESOURCES FOR FURTHER STUDY

Books and Articles

Farr, G. 1999. *Modern Iran*. New York: McGraw-Hill.

This short book approaches Iran from a sociological point of view. It discusses the major social institutions in Iran, including the family, religion, politics and the economy. In addition, it looks at the situation of women in modern day Iran. It also examines Iran's. growing problems of population growth and urban crowding.

Farman Farmain, Sattareh. 1992. *Daughter of Persia*. New York: Doubleday Press.

An Iranian woman writes this book. She describes her life from growing up in her father's harem to living through the Ira-

nian revolution. *The book shows the opulent life of the Iranian upper class, and the double life of women in Iran.*

Wright, Robin. 2000. *The Last Great Revolution: Turmoil and Transformation in Iran.* New York: Knopf.

One cannot understand modern Iran without understanding the Iranian revolution of 1979 and its causes and consequences. This is the best book to date on this powerful revolution. It explains why the Iranian people took to the streets to drive out the Shah and his followers and how the Shi'a Islamic clergy were able to seize to reins of the revolution and come to control Iran.

Websites

Iran Index
http://www.iranindex.com/

This website is a portal into the Iranian Internet with a search engine designed to find Iranian links.

Iran Press Service
http://www.iran-press-service.com/

This website was established in 1980 to provide an independent and objective news coverage of Iran. Reader beware, there is no such thing as objective news in the Middle East.

Islamic Republic Iran Broadcasting
http://www.irib.com/

This is the Iranian governments official news site.

Embassy of the Islamic Republic of Iran
http://www.ncf.carleton.ca

Believe it or not, although this is the website of the Iranian Embassy in Canada, there is still not one in the United States, this is a good website with useful information and links.

Films and Videos

An introduction to Iranian culture, by Shahnaz Moslehi. Canoga Park, CA: Eqbal Printing & Publishing (1994).

This documentary looks at the psychology of Iranians as well as Iranian immigrants to America. This film also delves into the Iranian way of life by looking at Iran's social life and customs, and takes the viewer into Iran's past.

SOUTH AFRICA

BASIC DATA

Population	43,426,386
Population Growth Rate	1.32%
Per Capita GDP	$6,800
Life Expectancy at Birth	54.76 Years
Form of Government	Republic
Major Religions	Christian 68%, Muslim 2%, Hindu 1.5%, Traditional and Animistic 28.5%
Major Racial and Ethnic Groups	Black 75.2%, White 13.6%, Coloured 8.6%, Indian 2.6%
Colonial Experience	Dutch and British Colony
Principal Economic Activities	Services 35%, Agriculture 20%, Industry 20%

INTRODUCTION

South Africa, officially the Republic of South Africa, is located at the southern-most tip of the African continent and borders the Atlantic and southern Indian Oceans to the west, south, and east. South Africa is slightly less than twice the size of Texas, and contains a population of over 43 million people. The Prince Edward and Marion Islands also make up South Africa's territory and are located to the southeast of Cape Town in the Atlantic (these islands were annexed in 1947). South Africa is a Republic that contains the executive, legislative, and judicial branches of government. The legislative branch consists of the National Assembly where members are elected by popular vote under a system of proportional representation. The president, who is also elected in a popular national vote, acts as both chief of state and head of government. In addition, there are three cities in South Africa that have been designated capitals in which each assumes a different branch of government; Pretoria, the administrative capital, Cape Town, the legislative, and Bloemfontein, the judicial capital.

South Africa's climate is semiarid, except along the east coast where the climate is subtropical. South Africa has been susceptibility to prolonged droughts. The terrain consists mainly of narrow coastal plains with a vast interior plateau surrounded by rugged hills. Reflecting South Africa's diversity, there are eleven official languages, which include Afrikaans, English, Ndebele, Pedi, Sotho, Swazi, Tsonga, Tswana, Venda, Xhosa, and Zulu.

SOUTH AFRICAN SOCIETY

Like most of the countries of the African Continent, the modern country of South Africa is the creation of European colonialism. Most of Africa was not colonized by Europe until the second half of the 19th Century. South Africa was the exception, largely because it was an important stopping off point for European ships sailing around the Horn of Africa to East Asia. In 1652, the Dutch established a permanent refueling station at the Cape, now Cape Town. Over the years this outpost expanded and the areas become a Dutch colony.

As more Dutch arrived and the colony grew, the Dutch began to develop agriculture and move north to homestead large tracts of land. The Dutch settlers in South Africa were called Afrikaans. The Dutch also began using local Africans for slave labor. In addition, since many of the early Dutch farmers were single men, African women were forced into concubinage. This union eventually created a distinctive racial group in South Africa, officially labeled Coloured.

In 1795 the British seized control of many of the Dutch territories around the world during the French revolutionary wars, including South Africa. Over the next hundred years, the British managed to assert control over much of the South African territory. Southern Africa had quickly become known for its rich minerals, and the discovery of diamonds and gold near the confluence of the Orange and Vaal rivers stimulated the flight of European prospectors to claim these lands. This northern push by the Europeans brought them into contact with more powerful African groups, especially the Zulu, and resulted in a number of bloody wars between the Europeans and the Africans. Eventually, the superior firepower of the Europeans won out and Europeans took land that had belonged to African tribes.

The contention over land not only led to war between the Africans and Europeans, but between Europeans themselves. The British tried to contro

Northern expansion of Dutch settlers, called Boers or farmers in Dutch, in the later part of the 19th Century, resulting in the Anglo-Boer War of 1899–1902. Though Britain won the war, the Boers were granted a generous amount of power, creating a strong and lasting influence in South Africa's affairs.

Although apartheid, a system based on racial superiority and privilege, in this case white dominance over blacks, had already taken hold, it was not formally recognized as an institution until 1948 when the National Party assumed control of the government by winning a majority of seats on a minority of votes. To implement Apartheid, one strategy was to create homelands, sometimes called *Bantustans,* where black African tribes or nationality would be forced to live. Reminiscent of the United States policy of creating Indian Reservations in the 19th Century, these *Bantustans* were usually in marginal or unproductive areas of the country.

The Apartheid policy also sought enforcement of total segregation of the population according to race, which involved the sorting of people by racial categories. This was expedited through the Population Registration Act of 1950 that had classified all citizens into four racial groups. All South Africans were required to carry identification that identified them as white, black, coloured, or Asian. These racial categories determined where one could work, go to school, live, and play.

Apartheid officially ended in 1994 with both the resignation of the National Party government that was composed largely of White Afrikaans, and the popular elections that brought the Government of National Unity to power and elected Nelson Mandela as president. While this race stratified policy is officially over, racial issues continue to dominate South African society and politics. As a result of this legacy, South Africa is a heterogeneous collection of multiple religions, languages, ethnic and racial groups, each with their own status, history, and issues.

RACE AND ETHNICITY GROUPS

Black Africans, that is the original Africans, make up 75 percent of the population of South Africa. Blacks are not a single or united ethnic group, but consist of many tribal and ethno-linguistic groups, some quite different from each other. Some of the major African groups include the Xhosa, the Zulu, and the Swazi. Some of these groups have lived in the area that is South Africa for many centuries, others have moved south out of central Africa into this area more recently.

Whites, or South Africans of European heritage, compose slightly over thirteen percent of the population. The white South Africans are composed of two groups; English descendents and Dutch descendents. The Dutch South Africans, called Afrikaans, or sometimes Boers, farmers in Dutch, came to South Africa before the British. Their language, Afrikaans, a variant of the Dutch language, is still an official language of South Africa and the Dutch influence remains strong in parts of South African society. Those of English descent compose the other White South Africans, and now make a majority of the White population. While the Afrikaans have little connection to present day Holland, the English in South Africa continue to maintain contact with Great Britain and travel between the two countries is common. The English and the Dutch fought a bitter war with each other for the control of South Africa in the last Century.

Coloureds, people of mixed race, make up almost nine percent of the population. The Coloured population is the result of the mixing of the White and African peoples over several centuries. Under apartheid, the coloured population enjoyed greater rights and freedoms than did the Black population, but less than the White population. Since the South African white population has been composed of two different groups, the English and Dutch, likewise the Coloured population can be divided into those descended from Dutch-African unions and those descended from English-African unions. Those descendents from Dutch-African unions tend to speak Afrikaans and make up the largest percentage of the Coloured population, while the descendents of English-African unions speak English and associate with the English culture.

There is also a sizeable Asian community in South Africa, approximately three percent of South Africa's population. The Asian community is composed mostly of Asian Indians, who were brought by the British or having migrated on their own. There is also a number of ethnic Chinese among those South Africans listed as Asian. Here again, the Asians are not a united community. The Asian Indians are divided between those who are Hindus and those who are Moslems.

RELIGION

Christianity is the dominant religion of South Africa, comprising sixty-eight percent of the population. The two major Christian denominations reflect South Africa's colonial heritage and include the Dutch Reform Church and the Anglican Church. In recent years, Evangelical Christians have been active in South Africa and have won considerable converts. The Dutch Reform Church is a rather strict Calvinist version of Protestantism and still has ties to the Dutch Reform Church in Holland. The Dutch Reform Church remains the Church of choice for the Afrikaans and the Coloureds who associate with the Afrikaans culture. It does not have great appeal to other South Africans, however, because of its strict doctrines. The Anglican Church is associated with the Church of England, and has gained a greater following among the other South Africans, including the blacks. This is the Church of Bishop Tutu, a well known Anglican Clergy and leader of the Anglican Church in South Africa. Approximately 60 percent of the Black populations are Anglicans, as well as 40 percent of the Asian Indians.

A large number of Black South Africans, approximately 28 percent of all South Africans, continue to follow native religions. These religions involve traditional animistic beliefs, similar to other native religions found throughout Africa. Finally, there are small, but important, Hindu and Moslem communities found mostly in the larger cities among the Asian Indian populations.

ECONOMY

South Africa is the largest and most advanced economy in Africa. The U.S. Department of Commerce identified South Africa as on of the world's top ten "Big Emerging Markets". With this designation the U.S. recognizes South Africa's immense potential for American businesses. In addition, South Africa accounts for about seventy-five percent of the GDP for the southern African region, and about forty-five percent for the entire African continent. South Africa also has a diversified economy with manufacturing representing the largest portion of the economy and contributing twenty-six percent of the GDP. The other major economic sectors include mining, commerce, agriculture, and business services.

The South African economy, however, is still crippled by many of the problems that remain from Apartheid, especially large areas of poverty and the lack of economic opportunity by the disadvantaged groups. In 1996 South Africa created the Growth Employment and Redistribution Strategy (GEAR) aimed at making the economy more competitive both within the country and globally. This program seeks to improve South Africa's position in the global marketplace by creating tax incentives, implementing trade liberalization and tariff reform, increased infrastructure investment, the elimination of import surcharges on capital goods, and the privatization of state assets. South Africa has also joined the World Trade Organization.

Despite its potential, economic problems remain. Unemployment remains around 30 percent and is much higher among some groups, especially Black South Africans. Economic growth has been sluggish, with the GDP, a measure of the nation's economic output, growing by only 0.3 percent in 1998. The per capita GDP, a measure of the nation's economic output per person, was $6,800 in 1998, the highest in Africa, but the nation's wealth is unevenly distributed. The poorest 10 percent of the population receives only 1.4 percent of the national income, while the richest 10 percent receives 47.3 percent.

POPULATION

There are over 43 million people living in South Africa as of 1999, and the population continues to grow at 1.32% a year, a relatively high rate. A high birthrate and a large number of women in their reproductive years account for the high growth rate. The total fertility rate, the average number of children a woman will have at current fertility rates, is 3.09. Although high, the total fertility rate has fallen. It was 4.4 children per woman in 1975. The population growth rate, as in most developing countries, varies across groups. Fertility rates are lowest in the White population, which is actually declining, and highest among the Black population, which is growing.

South Africa has a life expectancy of approximately 53 for males and 57 for females. It also has an infant mortality rate of approximately 52, meaning that 52 children die in the first year of life for every 1000 born. This relatively high death rate reflects problems with basic sanitation and health care, which particularly affect the young. It also is a result of South Africa's growing crisis with HIV and AIDS.

It is estimated that 20 percent of the South African population is infected with the HIV virus. Unlike other diseases which strike mostly small children or the elderly, AIDS kills adults in the prime of their lives, and, at least in Africa, women as well as men. The AIDS crisis is lowering the life expectancy in South Africa, and in the next two decades will lead to tremendous loss of life and human suffering. The American government's Agency for International Development estimates that within 10 years the life expectancy in South Africa will be 35, a drop of twenty years or almost 50 percent. This devastation will leave a population of old people with few able bodied adults to support them.

Literacy rates, which is defined here as those 15 and over who can read and write, is approximately 82 percent for both males and females. Although literacy rates are high, attendance rates for formal education is low. According to a Census taken in 1996, among people aged twenty and over, 4 million have never attended school and 3.5 million had only attended primary school.

WOMEN IN SOUTH AFRICA

The role of women in South African society is interwoven with the racial stratification system. With each of the racial groups, women's status is determined by the norms and values of that group. However, women are also given status in the larger society concomitant to their gender and their race. White women, for instance, may play a lesser role in White society than do White men, but they have a higher position within the society than do African women. Black women, who make up the largest segment of women, suffer both because of the traditional roles of women in society, and because they are Black. In other words, they are seen as inferior not only for being Black, but also for being female.

During apartheid, women faced educational and economic limitations. Statistics from 1970 show that of 100 white girls who started grade six, 58 reached grade ten, and for black girls only 2 reached 10th grade for every 100 that started grade six. Black women were often barred from obtaining any type of formal education, and they were relegated to the lowest echelons of the labor force. The results of gender discrimination are still present today. In 1990, black women who constitute approximately 37 percent of all South Africans, constituted 21 percent of the university students, while white men, who make up only about 7 percent of South African society, were 33 percent of South Africa's university students.

In addition, in 1990 60 percent of black African women were in the labor force, compared to 23 percent of white women. But over 82 percent of the black women were in the service sector where the lowest paying jobs are located. In addition, within the service sector 88 percent of the black African women were classified as domestic workers. Most white women were in supervisory positions.

South African women also face a high level of domestic and sexual violence. Studies have found that physical violence, especially those that force women into sexual relations, has become so common that many in society, including some women, no longer see it as a problem. A research report on sexual violence that surveyed over 26,000 high school youth and thousands of adult women and men found that 8 out of 10 young men felt women were responsible for causing sexual violence. The study also found that more than fifty percent of the young women also agreed that in situations of sexual assault women were usually to blame. More disturbing, the study also showed that over half of the youth interviewed—both male and female—felt that forcing someone to have sex did not constitute sexual violence.

Many in the South African government are aware of the difficult situation for women. The Reconstruction and Development Program (RDP), an integrated economic policy framework for developing South Africa has as one of its goals the creation of a non-sexist society through programs of creating quotas for women in the public sector. The RDP has stipulated that women should hold 30 percent of all management positions in the public sector. In addition, South Africa has created both the Commission on Gender Equity and the Human Rights Commission. The role of these two bodies is to oversee and investigate discriminatory practices against women, and to redress any problems that still remain. By 1999, 28.4 percent of the seats in parliament were held by women, compared to 12.5 percent in the United States. United Nations data also showed that 17.4 percent of the administrators and managers in South Africa were women, and that women made up 47 percent of the professional and technical workers.

SOUTH AFRICAN IN THE MODERN WORLD

South Africa has gone through tremendous changes in the last decade. It has witnessed the ending of Apartheid and the election of its first black president. Yet many of the problems of the past remain, including racial prejudice and discrimination, high levels of poverty, growing levels of crime and violence, and now the HIV pandemic that threatens to overwhelm the country. Visitors to parts of Cape Town or other large cities will see a modern industrialized country with modern stores, well-dressed people, and the conveniences of a developed country. On the other hand, visitors to other parts of South Africa will see shantytowns in devastating poverty, with poor or no sanitation, high levels of violence, and tribal warfare reminiscent of the poorest third world country. The first picture is largely white, the latter largely black. Despite the end of Apartheid there continues to be two South Africas, one poor and Black, the other wealthy and white.

The challenge for South Africa is to merge these two worlds, to bring the races together in a way that lifts the majority black population without driving out or destroying the white population. The government has developed a plan to make this happen, but the obstacles are great. Unemployment and low levels of education continue to limit the black workers, while fear, racism, and cronyism continue to limit the white population. Add to this a high level of anger, mutual dislike and suspicion on both sides, wrought by decades of Apartheid. Apartheid is over, but it will take decades for South Africa to heal.

SUMMARY

South Africa occupies the southern tip of the African continent. It was first colonized by the Dutch as a refueling station for ships sailing to the Far East in the 16th Century and later taken over by the British. Although a majority of the people are black Africans, the white population controlled South Africa, mostly those of Dutch descent, until 1994. The white government instituted a policy of racial stratification, called Apartheid, in which the people of South Africa were categorized into four racial groups, each with its own rights and statuses. South Africa has a population of over 43 million people and the population continues to grow. However, the disease of AIDS caused by the HIV virus threatens to kill millions of South African over the next decade resulting in a drastic fall in live expectancy. South Africa has also seen an increase in violence against women, especially but not limited to, forced sexual encounters and abusive relationships. This epidemic of violence against women has also abetted the AIDS crisis.

South Africa made history by overturning the rule of the Apartheid government and electing its first Black president. Nonetheless the challenges of bringing the country together remain staggering.

READING

Introduction

The following article, *Case Study: South Africa*, investigates the severe impact HIV/ AIDS has had on Africa, and South Africa in particular. While the rate of HIV infection grows exponentially, the South African government continues to deny just how large this problem really is. If this disease is left unchecked South Africa will suffer severe consequences both economically and socially. Not only will one's life expectancy drop to an average of forty years by 2008, a drop on average of twenty years, but also HIV/AIDS will overwhelm both the health and welfare systems, which potentially could create economic instability leaving fewer resources for other societal ills.

Reading

Case Study: South Africa, by Greg Barrow, BBC News.

Study Questions

1. What do you think globalization's role is in this HIV/AIDS epidemic? Note the article's discussion on compulsory licenses and how this runs counter to "free trade".

2. Why do you think women are more vulnerable to HIV/AIDS? Think of the section you just read on women in South Africa and their particular challenges in society?

3. While we know that HIV/AIDS affects all of society and that all of society is interconnected, can you think of any lasting effects HIV/AIDS will have on society that were not mentioned in this article? Think both on a local and global scale.

AIDS IN AFRICA: CASE STUDY: SOUTH AFRICA

By Greg Barrow

Every day, around 1500 people are newly infected with HIV in South Africa. Four million people are already HIV-positive, and there is no sign that the rate of infection is slowing down.

But at a time when Aids and HIV infection pose a grave threat to the country's future economic development, the government has blocked the provision of anti-Aids, or anti-retroviral drugs in the public health service, and has opened up a debate over whether HIV actually causes Aids.

This mind-boggling policy has been condemned by many scientists in the international community, but the voice of protest has been disturbingly quiet inside South Africa.

Dr Costa Gazi, the health spokesman for the tiny opposition party, the Pan Africanist Congress of Azania, is one exception.

The son of Greek immigrants to South Africa, Dr Gazi was jailed for his opposition to the apartheid regime in the 1960s, and then spent 20 years in exile in Britain. With his flowing grey hair, and Chicago Bulls baseball cap pulled low over his brow, he cuts an eccentric figure—but on the subject of Aids and HIV infection Dr Gazi has become a voice of clarity.

His call is simple: provide anti-Aids, or anti-retroviral drugs to pregnant mothers and tens of thousands of unborn babies can be protected from HIV infection. It's a call that the government has chosen to ignore.

"All we've had is a series of excuses," he says.

"They started by saying that anti-retroviral drugs are too expensive, then they were toxic, then they said we must examine the whole science of Aids. There's no seriousness on the side of the government, except that they don't want to spend more money on public health."

The voices of black patients from the township of Mdantsane, echo down the bare corridors of the Cecilia Makiwane hospital in the city of East London where Dr Gazi works. Named after South Africa's first black nurse, under apartheid it used to be the blacks-only hospital. In the new South Africa it has remained that way—a decrepit building of crumbling walls and leaking roofs, where open drains carry dirty water past overcrowded wards.

The metal gates that bar entry to the wards in the Cecilia Makiwane hospital are there to stop criminals stealing blankets and medicine. Poverty is so widespread in East London, that even the dying are not safe from the hands of thieves.

The hospital is desperately under-resourced, and now it is becoming increasingly overburdened by patients suffering from opportunistic illnesses associated with their HIV status. Dr Gazi believes there is a strong argument for the provision of anti-retroviral drugs because of the impact they would have in cutting the transmission of HIV from pregnant mothers to their unborn babies.

He has gone so far as to buy his own supplies of the anti-retroviral, Nevirapine, and intends to use it in the hospital. It's a move that is getting him into trouble with the local health authorities.

"They are threatening to punish me again," he says.

"But I'm going ahead anyway. The dispensary here is keeping its own supply of Nevirapine. I'm bringing it in to give it to them. We have to have good security because this is going to be popular stuff. You give the Nevirapine to women in la-bour, and then three drops are given to the baby after birth, and that's it! One tablet for the mother, three drops for the baby, end of story! You can save half the babies that would have been born with HIV."

It seems to be a simple argument in favour of the anti-retroviral drugs, but the ruling African National Congress says it cannot afford to pay for them and blames the international pharmaceutical companies for seeking to profit from Africa's Aids crisis.

There are, however, legal mechanisms the government could employ to secure a right to produce its own cheap anti-retrovirals.

If it can demonstrate that the drugs are required to contain a medical emergency, under the laws governing international trade, the government could seek what is known as a compulsory licence. Dr Gazi believes those conditions do exist.

"We have four million people who are HIV-positive," he says.

"At this moment, the number of deaths per day is going up very rapidly. This is a dire emergency, so anything that can be done to stem the progress of the epidemic, must be done.

"The anti-retroviral drugs will slow it down considerably, so I believe that this government can and should be issuing compulsory licences as of now. Also, we should be importing drugs…from countries that are making these drugs as a generic drug—countries like India and the Philippines.

"If not, we should be paying the price these companies are selling at today because even at today's prices, this is a cost-effective therapy."

Dr Gazi points out that the alternative to drug treatment is caring for sick children in homes—for as long as they remain alive—which according to some estimates would cost 10 or 20 times as much.

One possible explanation for the government's lack of enthusiasm for making anti-retroviral drugs available in the public health service is that it does not want to upset its economic ally, the United States.

If the government was to begin the process of issuing compulsory licences, it

would send the wrong signal to potential foreign investors. The licences undermine the principle of free trade, and they would set an uncomfortable precedent in a developing country.

But while these principles are pondered, the deadly impact of HIV in South Africa is rapidly increasing.

Statistics

- The annual anonymous unlinked survey of women attending public health antenatal clinics showed that 22.8% were HIV positive by the end of 1998
- This is a 33.8% increase on the 1997 figure
- The infection rate in young women aged 15–19 had increased from 12.7% in 1997 to 21% in 1998
- There is considerable variation in provincial figures ranging from 32.5% prevalence in KwaZulu-Natal to 5.2% in the Western Cape
- The rate of increase is highest in the Northern Province
- While there are limitations in extrapolating to the general population, it is estimated that 3.6 million South Africans were HIV positive in 1998, compared to approximately 2.7 million in 1997.
- This means about one in eight adult South Africans is HIV positive

What do these statistics mean?

- The epidemic in South Africa is serious and growing rapidly
- Young women are vulnerable
- We do not fully understand why some provinces are more affected than others and the clear provincial (and within-

province) variations need further epidemiological study
- Existing prevention programmes appear not to be working
- There is an urgency to reduce the number of new HIV infections and to manage the impact of existing infections on individuals, communities and organisations

Dynamics of the South African epidemic

The South African epidemic is exacerbated by:

- social and family disruption as a consequence of apartheid and migrant labour
- high mobility and a good transport infrastructure, allowing spread of the virus
- high poverty and low education levels, resulting in more risk taking behaviour and commercial sex work
- a burdened and transforming health system
- an overwhelmed and inadequate welfare system
- high levels of sexually transmitted diseases (STD's)
- the low status of women in society and relationships, making it difficult for them to protect themselves in sexual relationships

- shifting social norms which permit high numbers of sexual partners
- a resistance to change high risk behaviours, often centred around notions of culture resistance to condom usage
- a lack of clear and non-judgmental information and services for young people and denial about teenage sexual activity
- significant denial of homosexuality in the black community and a history of poor government interventions for the gay community

Summary

South Africa has a complex interrelationship of multiple epidemics, a heterogeneous society in transition and a government struggling to meet the needs of a united South Africa emerging from years of social engineering Projections.

Anthony Kinghorn and Malcolm Steinberg of HIV Management Services report that: that projections indicate that within 3 years almost 250,000 South Africans will die of AIDS each year.

This figure will rise to more that 500,000 by 2008.

Average life expectancy is expected to fall from about 60 years to around 40 years between 1998 and 2008.

Impact

- HIV/AIDS will pose significant economic costs to business over time but the macro-economic impact is likely to be limited to a Gross Domestic Product (GDP) growth rate reduction of about 1% per annum
- HIV/AIDS care will become a substantial part of health care spending
- Tuberculosis (TB) services and cure rates could deteriorate seriously

- Women will become more burdened by bearing the brunt of infections and care of the infected
- The HIV epidemic will produce large numbers of AIDS orphans (by 2005 there will be nearly a million children under the age of 15 who will have lost their mothers to AIDS)
- Education will be affected through staff becoming infected and through increasing needs of affected and infected children
- Welfare will face the challenge of dealing with those debilitated by AIDS, the numbers of AIDS orphans and the increase in elderly whose adult children die prematurely
- The majority of South Africans will be affected by this epidemic as it impacts on family members, friend and colleagues
- Social and political instability may increase

Response

Response from the state

An AIDS Advisory Group was appointed in 1985 but a specific AIDS Programme infrastructure was only established in 1991, consisting mainly of a network of AIDS Training, Information and Counselling Centres.

In 1992 the National AIDS Co-ordinating Committee of South Africa (NACOSA) was established, consisting of concerned individuals, non-governmental organisations (NGO's), AIDS service organisations (ASO's), local, provincial and national government, the African National Congress (ANC) Health Secretariat, as well as representatives of business, unions and churches.

Its task was to develop a draft National AIDS Strategy.

This was consolidated within a National AIDS Plan and formally adopted by government in 1994.

Resource constraints have severely hampered the implementation of the plan.

Responsibility for co-ordinating South Africa's response rests with the Directorate: HIV/AIDS & STDs in the Department of Health.

The core plan has remained the same but additions have included the "Beyond Awareness Campaign" and the "Partnership Against AIDS" strategy.

The Beyond Awareness Campaign is a multi-media multi-activity communications campaign from November 1998 to October 2000 run for the Directorate by a consortium of organisations involved in the HIV epidemic.

An Interministerial Committee on HIV/AIDS was established in parliament in 1997.

The 'Partnership Against AIDS' was launched on 9 October 1998 by the then Deputy President Thabo Mbeki to mobilise all South Africans to commit to working together around HIV/AIDS.

Mobilisation is largely carried out through events on action days (such as World AIDS Day).

Response from the NGO sector

There has been a significant NGO and ASO response to the epidemic, and a comprehensive network of organisations exists around South Africa.

This response has been greater in the bigger cities but there are problems with capacity and a drop in donor support since the advent of a democratic government.

The National Association of People With AIDS (NAPWA) has become a more powerful voice for those living with the virus.

A Treatment Action Campaign has been established to lobby for anti-virals to be more accessible to South Africans.

Response from the Human Rights community

A strong human rights campaign around HIV/AIDS emerged in the last decade leading to the development of the AIDS Legal Network, initiated by the AIDS Law Project at the Centre for Applied Legal Studies at the University of the Witwatersrand.

Some important landmark judgements around confidentiality and HIV testing have increased awareness of issues around HIV and the law.

The AIDS and the Law manual has assisted with the promotion of a human rights culture around HIV/AIDS.

Future Action

Kinghorn and Steinberg make the following comments:

- The results of campaigns and prevention programmes has been largely disappointing but an understanding of the key components of effective programmes has grown dramatically
- Lessons from other parts of Africa, especially Uganda and Tanzania, need to be taken on board
- More detailed understandings of the epidemiology of HIV in South Africa need to be developed to guide prevention programmes
- Socio-economic development must be accelerated
- Intersectoral co-ordination must be improved
- Strategic choices must be made
- Workplace programmes must be improved
- The health sector response must be strengthened

- Stigma around HIV/AIDS needs to be further reduced
- Support for the infected and affected needs urgent attention
- Improving the status of women is a priority
- Information of the epidemic and its impact must be spread more widely

- Life skills programmes for youth need to be fast tracked
- Consideration should be given to the prevention of maternal transmission
- Attention should be given to areas where infection rates are still low, people in risk situations and those whose sexual behaviour is not yet established

RESOURCES FOR FURTHER STUDY

Books and Articles

Gay, Phillip. 2001. *Modern South Africa*. New York: McGraw-Hill.

This book is part of a series on various countries written for sociology students. Chapters cover the major social institutions in South Africa, including chapters on the family, religion, the economy, and government. In addition, other chapters cover racial and ethnic issues, gender relations, and development issues. This is a good book for sociology students just beginning their study of South Africa.

Mandela, Nelson. 1995. *Long Walk to Freedom: The Autobiography of Nelson Mandela*. Waltham, Maryland: Little Brown and Co.

This is the autobiography of one of the most important people in the 20th Century and surely the most important person in the history of South Africa. After spending several decades in prison, he emerged to become president of his country and to see the end of Apartheid. Written mostly when he was behind bars, the book is largely about his thoughts and views, rather than a history of events and dates.

Mathabane, Mark. 1998. *Kaffir Boy: The True Story of a Black Youth's Coming of Age in Apartheid South Africa*. New York: Touchstone Books.

This book tells the story of Mark Mathabane who grew up in abject poverty during Apartheid in South Africa. He lived in South Africa's cruelest ghetto, where bloody gang war and midnight police raids were his education. Yet he was somehow able to gain an education and lift himself and his family out of poverty.

Pakenham, Thomas. 1992. *The Boar War*. New York: Avon Books.

This book is a detailed and dense, although readable, discussion of the Boar War between the Dutch settlers and the British. In this war, Europeans fought with each other over the control of African territory. This war was pivotal in South Africa's history.

Thompson, Leonard. 1996. *A History of South Africa*. New Haven: Yale Press.

This book is written by one of the leading scholars on South Africa and offers a readable and scholarly history of the country. It focuses primarily on the experiences of the black inhabitants rather on the white minority, as most histories do. The book does not cover the period after the end of Apartheid.

Websites

Welcome to South Africa
http://usaembassy.southafrica.net/

This is the official website of the South African Embassy in the United States. It has useful information on South Africa, the government, and the economics. It also has visa and travel information.

South African Statistics Home Page
http://www.statssa.gov.zu/

This is also an official site of the South African government. It has official statistics for South Africa and includes such things as the latest census data, economic output, schooling, etc. A very useful site.

South Africa Online
http://www.southafrica.co.za/

This website is a portal into the South African Internet. It has very useful general information on South Africa, but also links to other websites.

South Africa: Can A Country Overcome Its History
http://www.learner.org/exhibits/southafrica/
Annenberg/CPB/Multimediacollection

This is a website to the Annenberg Exhibit on South Africa that was part of a Public Broadcasting series on Africa. This site offers very good general history and description regarding South Africa. It is a good site for those just getting started in the study of South Africa.

Films and Videos

Mandela, Tambo, and the African National Congress: The struggle against apartheid, 1948–1990: a documentary survey, by S. John and R. Hunt Davis. New York; Oxford University Press (1991).

This documentary deals with apartheid, it's history, and the politics and government that was both complicit in supporting apartheid and that government which fought against it i.e. the African National Congress. The film also pays tribute to two of the most important people in SouthAfrica's freedom, Oliver Tambo and Nelson Mandela.

INDONESIA

BASIC DATA

Population	216,108,345
Population Growth Rate	1.46%
Per Capita GDP	$2,830
Life Expectancy at Birth	62.92 Years
Form of Government	Republic
Major Religions	Muslim 88%, Protestant 5%, Roman Catholic 3%, Hindu 2% Buddhist 1%
Major Racial and Ethnic Groups	Javanese 45%, Sundanese 14%, Madurese 7.5%, Coastal Malays 7.5%
Colonial Experience	Dutch Colony until 1950
Principle Economic Activity	Agriculture 18.8%, Industry 40.3%, Services 40.9%

INTRODUCTION

Indonesia, officially the Republic of Indonesia, is a country in South East Asia, consisting of the Islands in the Indonesian archipelago. Indonesia stretches almost 5000 kilometers from the Asian mainland into the Pacific Ocean and forms a bridge between the Pacific and the Indian Ocean. The country consists of over 17,000 islands, the largest being Sumatra, Java/Mandura, Kalimantan (which comprises two-thirds of the Island of Borneo), Sulawesi, and Irian Jaya (which makes up part of the Island of New Guinea).

The population of Indonesia is over 216 million, the fourth largest in the world. In total landmass, Indonesia is approximately three times the size of Texas. The capital is Jakarta. There are over 500 different ethnic groups in Indonesia, and over 500 languages or dialects are spoken. The official language is Bahasa Indonesian, a Malay language similar to the languages spoken in Malaysia and the Philippines.

INDONESIAN SOCIETY

Like many of the countries in the third world, Indonesia is largely the creation of European colonists, mostly the Dutch. European interests in this area began when the Portuguese explorer Vasco de Gama visited the area in 1497–1499. Europe was interested in the spices found in this area, particularly nutmeg, mace, and cloves, which were used in Europe to cure meat in the days before refrigeration. While profits were the chief motive for exploring this area, the Catholic Papacy had also charged Portugal with converting Asia to Christianity.

The Dutch, who began to colonize the Islands as well as the Malay Peninsula, soon followed the Portuguese. Although it took them several hundred years, the Dutch eventually colonized all of the area that is now Indonesia and ruled, except for a brief period of English rule, until the Japanese occupation during WWII. The Dutch cultural influence in Indonesia is still strong in some areas, as is the Indonesian influence in the Netherlands.

Holland attempted to regain control of the Islands after WWII, but Indonesia declared itself an independent country and resisted Holland's return to power. By 1950, Holland conceded Indonesia's independence, and Indonesia officially became an independent country. The first leader of Indonesia was Sukarno, who ruled from 1945 to 1967. Suharto who ruled Indonesia from 1967 to 1998 followed him.

The challenge of making a nation out of 16,000 Islands and over 500 different ethnic groups has been considerable. Within Indonesia is a large diversity of people, lifestyles, religions, languages, and economies. Although Moslems make up a majority of the population, there are also populations of Buddhists, Hindus, and Christians. It has the largest rain forest in Asia. In some areas people continue to live in small hunting and gathering bands, while in the major cities people live modern urban lives. This diversity has led to secessionist demands and has sparked armed uprisings in several areas.

RELIGION

Indonesia is the largest Moslem country in the world. Approximately 88 percent of the population is Moslem, with small populations of Christians, Hindus and

Buddhist. It is not known exactly how Islam came to Indonesia; Arab traders probably brought it to the Islands in the 14th Century. When Islam arrived, many of the people of Indonesia were Hindus or Buddhists, and local animist religions also existed.

While the Moslems in Indonesia follow the major tenets of the Islamic faith, the Islam practiced in Indonesia is somewhat different than the rest of the Islamic world. As Islam came to the Islands, the local people created their own syncretic version of Islam, mixing in local beliefs and customs. This can be seen in several ways. In some parts of Indonesia, particularly Java, a form of Islam is practiced called *kebatinan,* which combines Islam with animism, Hindu-Buddhism, and ancestor worship. President Suharto was an adherent of *kebatinan.*

The Islam practiced in Indonesia is also not as strict as orthodox Islam on rules that constrain women's behavior. In pre-Islamic Indonesian culture, women played important roles in the society. As a result, Indonesian women play a more active role in their society than do women in most other Islamic countries.

Hinduism existed in Indonesia before Islam and is found principally on the Island of Bali. As with Islam, the Balinese have modified orthodox Hinduism, mixing it with local customs and beliefs. Balinese Hinduism does not follow the traditional Hindu focus on the cycles of rebirth and reincarnation, but rather puts emphasis on acts of ritual purity and the worship of local ancestors and spirits. The Balinese dance ceremonies and puppet plays acting out these rituals are well known in the West.

Christianity is also found in Indonesia and Christians are growing in number. Some early Catholic communities can be traced back the Portuguese presence in the 16th Century, and the Dutch converted a small number of Indonesians to Protestantism during several centuries of their rule. The Dutch colonist, however, was largely secular, and so was not interested in converting natives to Christianity. In addition, the Dutch religion was a strict and forbidding version of Calvinism that had little appeal to the native Indonesians. It was not until Lutheran, and later Catholic, missionaries appeared after 1900 that Christianity began to spread in Indonesia, particularly in the undeveloped areas of Irian Jaya and Timor. More recently, fundamentalist Christian missionaries, funded by large western religious organization, have been active in parts of Indonesia. These missionaries have been successful in converting large numbers of Indonesians to fundamentalist Christianity and have created growing hostility on the part of the Islamic leaders.

INDONESIAN ETHNIC GROUPS

Indonesia is made up of numerous ethnic groups. These can be divided into those groups who are indigenous to Indonesia and ethnic minorities who have immigrated to Indonesia. No group constitutes a statistical majority. Javanese are the largest ethnic group in Indonesia and constitute approximately 45 percent of the Indonesian population. The Javanese live in east and central

Java, and on the Islands of Sumatra, Sulawesi, and Kalimantan. The Javanese form the political elite in Indonesia and most of the countries leaders and generals are Javanese. While the Javanese are proud of their culture and society, their life and identity is centered on the village, rather than on kin or tribe. With a strong sense of local traditions and culture, the Javanese have been resistant to Islamic conversions.

As with other Indonesian groups, the Javanese trace their family ties on both the male and female side. As a result, Javanese women can play an important role in family and village life. Javanese also largely disregard Islamic proscriptions regarding women's veiling or the separation of the genders in public.

The second largest group is the Sundanese, who live in West Java. They constitute approximately 14 percent of the population of Indonesia. The Sundanese language is related to Javanese, but cannot be mutually understood. The Sundanese culture and social structure is similar to that of the Javanese in which both have strong village ties and gender egalitarian linage systems. However, the Sundanese have been more eager to take to orthodox Islam, although their religious practices also contain some traces of animism and Hinduism.

The best known ethnic group, at least outside of Indonesia, is the Balinese. The Balinese count about 2.5 million and they are largely the inhabitants of the Islands of Bali, Lombok, and the western half of Sumbawa. The Balinese have a strong sense of their own ethnic identity. They are well known in the larger world as stately, aesthetically inclined people with rich traditional customs and arts. They are fiercely anti-Moslem, and have maintained their Hindu religion in the face of considerable pressure to convert to Islam.

There are numerous other ethnic groups in Indonesia including the people of Sumatra, the Acehnese, the Batak, and the Minangkabau. All of these groups have some cultural and societal similarity to the other indigenous peoples of Indonesia. Their populations are relatively small, particularly compared to the Javanese and Sundanese, but several of these groups, particularly the Acehnese and the Batak, have wielded considerable influence on the history of Indonesia largely in their attempts to form independent territories.

MINORITY GROUPS

There are a number of non-Indonesia ethnic groups living in Indonesia. These include the Toraja in central Sulawesi, the Dayak in southern Kalimantan, the Weyewa in the Western highlands of Sumba, the Tanimbarese in the southern part of the Maluka Province on the Island of Sumatra, the Asmat in the south-central alluvial swamps of Irian Jaya, and the Chinese who live in many areas of Indonesia, but mostly in the large cities. All of these groups have faced periods of discrimination and prejudice in Indonesia, but the group that has faced the greatest discrimination in the modern period has been the Chinese.

The Chinese are not one distinct group, but represent populations that came from southern China over the last several centuries. In some areas of Indonesia the Chinese live apart in "Chinatowns", while in other areas of Indonesia they have mixed with the local people. Indonesia does not attempt to enumerate the Chinese in its census, but it is estimated that there are at least 10 million people in Indonesia who identify as being Chinese. The Chinese have been successful in the business sector of Indonesia society, both as small shop owners, but also as successful businessmen in national corporations. Chinese businessmen control a large portion of Indonesia's economy, to the discomfort of many Indonesians. This has led to the scapegoating of Chinese and a number of anti-Chinese riots have taken place in Indonesia.

The Chinese in Indonesia have also at times been punished for the actions of China, which they had nothing to do with. Major anti-Chinese riots occurred in December of 1965 when Chinese were blamed for the involvement of the Indonesian Communist party in the failed Coup of 1965. It was thought that China had promoted the Coup, but most Indonesian Chinese had nothing to do with either the Coup, nor the Communist party, nor even with China. But rioter who killed many Chinese in 1965 ignored this detail. It is estimated that somewhere around 300,000 Chinese were killed in 1965, the bloodiest event in postwar Southeast Asia until the Khmer Rouge killings in Cambodia a decade later.

Anti-Chinese riots again took place in Indonesia in 1998, when Chinese merchants were blamed for Indonesian's economic collapse. The number of causalities is not known, but many small Chinese shop owners were attacked and blamed for the economic downturn.

POPULATION TRENDS

Indonesia has the fourth largest population in the world and although the growth rate has slowed, the population continues to grow. The United Nations Development Programme estimates that Indonesia's population will reach 250 million by the year 2015. The rapid population growth rate is a result of two factors, a large number of women in their childbearing years, coupled with a high birthrate. The total fertility rate in Indonesia, the number of children a woman will have over her lifetime at current birthrates, is estimated to be 2.57 (1999). As a result, the Indonesian population is growing at an annual rate of 1.46 percent. However, the growth rate has been slowing. For instance, the total fertility rate in 1975 was almost five children per women. This slow down in the growth rate is caused by the improvement in the Indonesian economy in the last two decades, the increased educational opportunities for women, and the later age of marriage. However, the population will still continue to grow because of the high number of women of childbearing years.

Indonesia has a high infant mortality rate relative to other countries at the same level of development, estimated to be 57.3 deaths of children under the age of one year in 1999 for every 1000 lives births. The infant mortality rate is a key indicator of the general health of a country, since young children are the most susceptible to disease or environmental pollution. Indonesia's high infant mortality rate is indicative of a society with a large scattered rural population where health services are scarce. The high infant mortality rate may also indicate high levels of crowding in some urban areas and the lack of proper sanitation services, especially clean water. Also related to the general health of a society is life expectancy. In Indonesia, males can expect to live 61 years on the average, and females over 65 years.

With a high birth rate, Indonesia has a high proportion of its population less than 15 years of age at 30 percent of the population. On the other hand, the percentage of the population over 65 years of age is just 5 percent. As a result, Indonesia will have plenty of workers to support the older generations in the future. However, the key will be to find jobs for the growing number of youth entering the labor market.

With its large population and limited land area, crowding is a problem in some areas of Indonesia. Crowding problems, however, are concentrated in specific areas, particularly the Island of Java. Java has approximately 7 percent of the total land area of Indonesia, but 60 percent, or over 107,000,000 people, reside in Java. This gives Java a population density of over 800 people per square kilometer, one of the most dense areas in the world. On the other hand, the Island of Kalimantan represents 28.10 percent of the area of Indonesia with a population of slightly over 9 million, and has a density of 17 people per square kilometer. The least dense areas of Indonesia are found on Irian Jaya, which is part of the Island of New Guinea. Irian Jaya makes up 22 percent of the landmass of Indonesia, but with only a little over 1.5 million people it has a density of 4 people per square kilometer. In comparison, the state of New Jersey, the most densely populated state in the United States, has 382 people per square kilometer, while Alaska, the least dense, has .33 people per square kilometer.

ECONOMY

Before 1997, the Indonesian economy was considered one of the success stories in the world. Indonesia had grown rapidly during the early 1990's and had seen a sharp rise in manufacturing, exports, economic growth, and in the general standard of living. This rapid economic expansion had been the result of global investments into Indonesia, primarily by the Japanese, creating factories and assembly plants that produced products for the world markets. In addition, Indonesia was a major supplier to the world of raw materials, including oil, rubber, and lumber.

In 1997 and 1998, this economic growth collapsed. In 1997 the rupiah, the Indonesian currency, dropped in value, and inflation reach 77 percent by 1998. In 1998 alone, Indonesia's economic output, measured by the GDP, fell almost 14 percent. Foreign investors removed their money from Indonesia, factories closed, the unemployment rate jumped, and major civil unrest occurred. In the ensuing riots Chinese businessmen were attacked and by May of 1998, only three months after being selected for a seventh five-year term, president General Suharto resigned from office. By 2000 the economy had improved again with the help of the IMF and other world financial institutions, but the damage of 1997–1998 is still present.

The United Nations ranks Indonesia as a "medium human development" country. This means that according to a number of economic, human rights, and developmental statistics, Indonesia is in the middle. The per capita GDP, an indirect measure of average income, is estimated to be $2,830 for 1998. Indonesia's unemployment rate is reported to be over 20 percent, but it is no doubt higher in many areas. Also, like many third world countries, Indonesia has a highly unequal income distribution; the poorest 10 percent of the population receives about 3.6 percent of the national income, while the richest 10 percent receive 28 percent of the income.

MODERNIZATION

Like many third world countries, modernization and globalization present a number of challenges to Indonesia. Because Indonesia is physically a series of Islands, and culturally made up of many ethnic and linguistic groups, the problems of bringing these various parts into a national culture remain. In addition, the recent economic collapse has made Indonesia wary of opening up its economic borders to the global market place, yet not to do so also has its costs. Finally, Indonesia is a Moslem country, albeit on the periphery of the Islamic world, and it seeks to protect or shield its peoples from the corrupt influences of Western culture and social values. The Moslem leaders are particularly bothered by the recent incursion of Christian missionaries.

Indonesia also faces the threat of secessionist movements in several of its more remote areas where the local people do not want to be part of Indonesia and seek their independence. These areas include Timor, which received world attention in 1998, the Toraja in central Sulawesi, and the Dayak in southern Kalimantan. In most cases these people were brought into the nation of Indonesia by force and they want out.

Globalization also presents modern Indonesia with other problems associated with modern lifestyles. Computers, telephones, and television are changing the social landscape of Indonesia. People are connected around the world and therefore better informed. As the mass demonstrations of 1998 showed, Indonesians want a better lifestyle, and a more representative government. They are not willing to tolerate the cronyism and corruption of the past. These forces are shaping a new Indonesia. Time will tell if the government can keep up with its people

SUMMARY

Indonesia is a country created by European colonialist, most the Dutch. The country is a series of Islands in South Asia with a population of over 217 million, the fourth larges population in the world. Indonesia is made up of many groups, languages, and religions. A majority of the population are Moslems. Indonesia became independent after WWII. The Javanese make up about 45 percent of the population, followed by the Sundanese, and the Balinese. There also a number of minorities in Indonesia, the largest group being the Chinese who have suffered from prejudice and discrimination. Many Chinese have been killed in anti-Chinese riots.

Indonesian families tend to balance male and female lineages and women play an important role in the traditional and modern society. As one of the largest countries in the country, Indonesia faces crowd-ing in some areas. The population will continue to grow, but the birthrate has begun to decrease. The most important event in Indonesia in last decade has been the collapse of the Indonesian economy and resulting social and political unrest.

Indonesia faces many of the same problems developing countries face. Economic and social development remain a challenge, population growth must be slowed, and a national society and culture is still evolving. Increasingly active secessionist movements among marginalized groups will pose a problem to national solidarity in the decades to come.

READING

Introduction

The following article, *The Fragile Archipelago,* is from the BBC on the current situation in Indonesia. It especially focuses on the difficulty of creating a united country out of thousands of Islands and hundreds of ethnic groups. Recent ethic troubles have occurred in East Timor, where the East Timorese, who are mostly Catholics, voted for independence. The Indonesian government in Jakarta did not allow them to secede and the Indonesian Army crushed their independence movement. The area of Aceh has also demanded independence.

Reading

The Fragile Archipelago, by Catherine Napier, BBC News.

Study Questions

1. What are the major obstacles Indonesia faces in creating a united country? How does its colonial history help or hinder the process of creating a united country?
2. If you were the president of Indonesia would you grant independence to Aceh and East Timor? Why?

THE FRAGILE ARCHIPELAGO

By former Jakarta Correspondent Catherine Napier

Indonesia's national motto is "Bhinneka tunggal" or "unity in diversity". It was coined by the leaders of the new Republic proclaimed in 1945 and the political challenge it reflects is as true today as it was more than 50 years ago.

For although half a century of being part of an independent Indonesia has led to a strong sense of national identity across the more than 13,000 islands that make up the archipelago, many other forces still pulling the country apart.

The declaration of independence followed a slow process of Dutch colonisation which began in the 17th century with the creation of the Dutch East India Company.

It was spices which attracted European traders to a small collection of islands in what is now Eastern Indonesia. The Dutch monopolised the trade and from there expanded their influence—largely through indirect rule—across the collection of independent sultanates and principalities which made up the region then.

Political unity under the Dutch was only achieved at the beginning of this century, leaving strong regional identities intact.

Forging a National Identity

It was Indonesians themselves who were left to confront the problem of how to unify a country of more than 250 ethnic groups, whose experience of the Dutch varied from region to region.

The war of independence against the Dutch, from 1945 to 1950, was of key importance in helping to forge a national identity, as was the post-colonial leadership under Sukarno and Hatta.

Sukarno, who became the first president of the Republic, was a supreme nationalist. It was he who invented Indonesia's national ideology of Pancasila designed to promote tolerance amongst diverse religious and ideological groups.

Preaching monotheism—belief in one god—and crucially Indonesian unity, it had few critics until later on when, under Indonesia's second President Suharto, Pancasila became a tool of state repression.

The spread of a national language—Bahasa Indonesia—also helped unify a multi-lingual population. Intermarriage helped, internal migration helped.

The consolidation of army power, the creation of internal security agencies and the general militarisation of society under President Suharto established a kind of order in which economic development flourished and challenges against the state were more or less doomed from the outset—until the economy collapsed and Suharto's rule with it.

But antagonism between the central most heavily populated island of Java and the outlying regions continues to present the most serious political challenge to the government even today.

After independence, President Sukarno faced a series of rebellions in the early 1950s led by disaffected army commanders and Islamic leaders. In 1950 a new—short lived—unitary constitution was adopted with a centralised administration in Jakarta.

Although politically dominant, Java was dependant on income from exports from the resource-rich outer islands and the Javanese were accused of exploitation.

This sort of grievance is still pulling Indonesia apart.

Demands for Independence

Aceh is a case in point. A strongly Islamic area which fought a war against the Dutch, Aceh has also been in regular conflict with the leadership of independent Indonesia.

Since the 1950s Aceh has been demanding greater autonomy, first supporting an Islamic rebellion against the state then later supporting an independence movement known as the Free Aceh Movement.

Aceh was granted the status of a special region in 1959 but the reality of life within the Indonesian republic has not been to the liking of most of its population.

Brutal counter-insurgency operations in the late 1980s and early 1990s alienated its inhabitants, further increasing support for the independence movement.

Sukarno soon ran into trouble with the new Indonesian state. A seven year experiment with democracy ended in 1957 with Indonesian unity in crisis.

Martial law was imposed and political life restricted, although in foreign policy Sukarno struck out as a fierce anti-colonialist and self-styled leader of an alliance of newly independent Afro-Asian states which later became the Non Aligned Movement.

Clash of Old and New

These states supported Sukarno's claim to Irian Jaya which he secured from the Dutch in 1969 after a period under UN supervision.

But for indigenous Papuans the history of the province since then has been a far from happy one. Treated as second class citizens, they have suffered the invasion of their tribal lands by developers and transmigrants while their natural resources are plundered for the benefit of Jakarta.

Perhaps nowhere in Indonesia is the clash of the old and new so apparent as the siting of a state of the art gold and copper mine—Freeport Indonesia—in a mountainous area populated by near stone age tribes.

President Suharto sent special combat troops to crush an independence movement—the Free Papua Organisation or OPM—but anti-Indonesian activity has increased in recent years and serious demands for independence have resurfaced.

As in other disaffected areas of the republic, the collapse of the Suharto regime has led to unrealistic expectations of change and a promised "dialogue" on autonomy has been postponed.

East Timor 'Special Case'

The end of Indonesian rule in East Timor, a former Portuguese colony invaded by Indonesia in 1975 is likely to further fuel such expectations. Since its incorporation into the Republic, East Timor's majority Catholic population had been subjected to sustained repression by the Indonesian army determined to crush separatist sentiment at the cost of many thousands of lives.

East Timor's vote for independence in a United Nations supervised ballot on autonomy has prompted real worries that other regions will be encouraged to to break away.

But East Timor has been a special case in the sense that the United Nations never accepted the Indonesian annexation of 1976.

Many Irianese feel they have an equally strong case for independence, but for other regions fed up with Jakarta it seems that at least part of the answer must lie in genuine decentralisation, a path the present interim government has already embarked upon.

RESOURCES FOR FURTHER STUDY

Books and Articles

Draine, Cathie and Barbara Hall, Eds. 1991. *Culture Shock!: Indonesia.* Portland, OR: Graphic Arts Center Publishing.

This book is designed for Indonesian travelers and expatriates living in Indonesia. It is part of a series of books for this purpose. However, despite its lightweight credentials, the book does have a useful description of Indonesian culture, values, and food, as well as a short but useful history. The book only covers Java, Sumatra, Bali, and Sulawesi.

Emmerson, Donald. 1999. *Indonesia Beyond Suharto: Polity, Economy, Society, Transition.* Armonk, NY: M. E. Sharpe Publishers.

This book is a reader of eleven different chapters on modern Indonesia written by experts in their fields. It includes chapters on the politics, the economy, the society, and on the transition after Suharto. It also includes section on women and religions. Indonesians write several of the chapters.

Schwarz, Adam. 1999. *A Nation in Waiting: Indonesia's Search for Stability.* Boulder, Colorado: Westview Press.

The author, Adam Schwarz, is a reported for the **Far Eastern Economic Review** and was stationed in Indonesia. This book covers the development of In-

donesia over the last 30 years from an impoverished agrarian set of Islands into a modern nation. The book primarily focuses on President Suharto and his style of leadership through cronies and family nepotism. Although the book was written while Suharto was still in power, the author nonetheless predicts the coming crisis that would oust Suharto in 1998.

Matthew, Jardine, Allan Nairn, Steve Cox, and Constancio Pinto. 1996. *East Timor's Unfinished Struggle: Inside the Timorese Resistance.* Cambridge, MA: South End Press.

This book looks at the struggle of the East Timorese for independence from Indonesia. This Catholic Portuguese speaking province has tried for some time to break away from the largely Islamic Indonesia. This book largely follows the plight of a 33-year-old Timorese man and his struggles.

Websites

Ministry of Foreign Affairs of The Republic of Indonesia
http://www/deplu.go.id/

This is the official Website for the Ministry of Foreign Affairs of the Indonesian government. This site features Indonesia's foreign policies, and links to missions abroad.

Inside Indonesia-Magazine
http://www.insideindonesia.org/

This is the site to a scholarly journal written by Indonesian intellectuals and scholars. The journal carries a number of interesting articles about various issues in Indonesia. One should be aware, however, that there is not complete journalistic nor academic freedom in Indonesia.

Indonesian Home Page
Http://indonesia.elga.net.id/

This website is maintained by the University of Manitoba, Canada. It is the best general Website on Indonesia and his general information about Indonesia, as well as other information on language, culture, history, and music.

Films and Videos

The Balinese people: A reinvestigation of character, by Gordon D. Jensen. Singapore; New York: Oxford University Press (1992).

This documentary on the Balinese people of Indonesia provides us with an exhaustive account of the Balinese way of life. The customs, social life, personalities, and culture are analyzed as well as the *psychological and mental health aspects of this unique society.*

Indonesian business culture, by Rob Goodfellow. Singapore: BH Asia (1997).

This film takes you inside the business culture of Indonesia with an emphasis on the proper etiquette and the particular ethics involved in Indonesian business. Religion, particularly Islam, also plays a large part in Indonesian society including business life. Islam, as well as the social and economic conditions of Indonesian society, are along with the overall depiction of Indonesian business life, all aspects of this film.